GRACED
TO GO

GRACED TO GO

STEP INTO
THE **BIGGER**
BOLDER LIFE
THAT BELONGS
TO YOU

VICTORIA OSTEEN

Faith
Words

New York • Nashville

FaithWords
Hachette Book Group
1290 Avenue of the Americas, New York, NY 10104
faithwords.com
@FaithWords / @FaithWordsBooks

First Edition: July 2025

FaithWords is a division of Hachette Book Group, Inc. The FaithWords name and logo are
trademarks of Hachette Book Group, Inc.

The publisher is not responsible for websites (or their content) that are not owned by
the publisher.

The Hachette Speakers Bureau provides a wide range of authors for speaking events. To find
out more, go to hachettespeakersbureau.com or email HachetteSpeakers@hbgusa.com.

FaithWords books may be purchased in bulk for business, educational, or promotional use.
For information, please contact your local bookseller or the Hachette Book Group Special
Markets Department at special.markets@hbgusa.com.

All Scripture quotations, unless otherwise indicated, are taken from the Holy Bible, New
International Version®, NIV®. Copyright ©1973, 1978, 1984, 2011 by Biblica, Inc.™ Used
by permission of Zondervan. All rights reserved worldwide. www.zondervan.com. The "NIV"
and "New International Version" are trademarks registered in the United States Patent and
Trademark Office by Biblica, Inc.™

Scripture quotations marked (ESV) are from The ESV® Bible (The Holy Bible, English
Standard Version®), © 2001 by Crossway, a publishing ministry of Good News Publishers.
Used by permission. All rights reserved.

Scripture quotations marked (MEV) are taken from THE HOLY BIBLE, MODERN
ENGLISH VERSION. Copyright © 2014 by Military Bible Association. Published and
distributed by Charisma House.

Library of Congress Cataloging-in-Publication Data

Names: Osteen, Victoria author
Title: Graced to go : step into the bigger bolder life that belongs to you
    / Victoria Osteen.
Description: First edition. | Nashville : Faith Words, 2025.
Identifiers: LCCN 2025004031 | ISBN 9781546010654 hardcover | ISBN
    9781546010647 ebook
Subjects: LCSH: Self-actualization (Psychology)—Religious
    aspects—Christianity | Self-actualization (Psychology)—Biblical
    teaching | Christian life | Christian life—Biblical teaching
Classification: LCC BV4598.2 .O889 2025 | DDC 158.1—dc23/eng/20250519
LC record available at https://lccn.loc.gov/2025004031

ISBN: 9781546010654 (hardcover), 9781546009283 (large print),
9781546010647 (ebook)

Printed in the United States of America

LSC

Printing 1, 2025

To God's amazing grace

CONTENTS

INTRODUCTION

You were never meant to live…stuck.

Yet so many of us feel precisely that way. Stuck in a job we don't love. Stuck in negative circumstances. Stuck in the safety of something that is familiar but far below what God wants for us.

So what is the key to getting un-stuck? As the title of this book hints, it's *grace*! That's God's favor and blessing to accomplish what you can't accomplish on your own and to overcome what should hold you back. Grace is not something you have to earn; it's a gift from God so you can fulfill your purpose. The word *grace* appears 146 times in the Scripture. Understanding grace and how it empowers us is vital to becoming who you were created to be.

It's significant that the word *Go* appears 1,542 times in the Bible, but the word *stay* only appears 62 times. God is much more interested in our *going* forward than our *staying* stuck.

From the beginning of the Bible to its final book, we see God calling and urging His people to get going. His marching orders to Adam and Eve were, "Be fruitful. Multiply. Go take possession of the earth. Cultivate and keep it." He basically said, "Here's a big wide world I've given you. Now go! Go experience increase. Go experience growth." When Moses led the Israelites to the edge of the land of promise, once again His marching orders were, "Go! I've given you this land. Now go take possession of it."

Notice Jesus' final words to His disciples right before ascending into Heaven:

> Then Jesus came to them and said, "All authority in heaven and on earth has been given to me. **Therefore go** and make disciples of all nations, baptizing them in the name of the Father and of the Son and of the Holy Spirit, and teaching them to obey everything I have commanded you. And surely I am with you always, to the very end of the age." (Matthew 28:18–20)

There's that word again. It's right there at the beginning of what is often called "The Great Commission." Jesus is saying, "When I call you to do something, I've graced you to do it. So, go!"

We see it again in the book of Acts in the salvation story of Saul, the future Apostle Paul. Saul had just been knocked down by the power and light of Jesus appearing to him. The encounter left him temporarily blinded. A few verses later, the Lord speaks to a man named Ananias about finding Saul and ministering to him:

In Damascus there was a disciple named Ananias. The Lord called to him in a vision, "Ananias!" "Yes, Lord," he answered. The Lord told him, "**Go** to the house of Judas on Straight Street and ask for a man from Tarsus named Saul, for he is praying." (Acts 9:10–11)

That was a scary "Go" for Ananias to hear. Saul had been harshly persecuting Jesus' followers and throwing them in prison. In fact, Saul was on his way to do some more persecuting when he encountered Jesus. Like Moses and so many of the other people God called throughout the Bible, Ananias is reluctant to step out and obey. Watch what happened next:

> "Lord," Ananias answered, "I have heard many reports about this man and all the harm he has done to your holy people in Jerusalem. And he has come here with authority from the chief priests to arrest all who call on your name."
>
> But the Lord said to Ananias, "**Go!** This man is my chosen instrument to proclaim my name to the Gentiles and their kings and to the people of Israel." (Acts 9:13–15)

Do you see it? This time God's "Go" was even more emphatic. "Go!" Read the rest of that chapter and you'll discover that Ananias obeyed, and everything turned out great. He got to play a key part in seeing Saul healed of blindness and being launched into his transformation, "the Apostle Paul," a man who changed the world and wrote nearly half of the books in the New Testament.

The same is true of you. God wants to use you to do amazing things. That's why I'm writing to encourage you that you're graced to go. Grace is not just God's kindness to you, it's divine power to enable you to do things you could never do in your own power.

Grace is supernatural favor that moves you into God's highest and best. When God extends grace, you accomplish far more than anyone—yourself included—could have expected. Grace is the power to overcome challenges and outlast opposition. It's the power to bounce back from setbacks and move forward.

....

Grace is supernatural favor that moves you into God's highest and best.

....

Jesus said, "In the world you will have tribulation. But be of good cheer. I have **overcome** the world" (John 16:33 MEV). So many people in the Bible demonstrate that truth.

Moses was a wanted fugitive from Egypt who didn't speak well and had no confidence. When God initially assigned him to be the one to lead the Israelites out of slavery in Egypt, he insisted to God that he wasn't the person for the job. But God graced him to go and confront the most powerful ruler in the world and lead more than a million Israelite slaves to freedom.

Hannah was childless and filled with shame about it, yet she stepped out in faith to pray. God's grace gave her a breakthrough that produced a son—the prophet Samuel. David was the youngest and least outwardly impressive of several brothers, yet God graced him to go and deliver his entire nation from the threat of Goliath, the warrior giant who taunted them.

The Bible is filled with the stories of hundreds of individuals who felt stuck in lives that felt small or fearful or common or just plain hard, and then God challenged them to trust Him for a bigger, better, and more extraordinary life. Their stories show us that when they trusted Him and took a step, God blessed them with grace to go. And as they stepped out, they found themselves doing things they could never have dreamed of doing. They found the Spirit of the Lord moving upon them to give them supernatural strength and ability. And here is wonderful news:

That was in the Old Testament. After Jesus came, died for our sins, ascended to Heaven, and then sent the Holy Spirit, we got a much better deal than Moses or David ever had. We not only have the Spirit of the Lord *upon* us,

He lives *within* us. Back then, the Spirit of the Lord would only rest upon God's people from time to time, but Jesus promised that the "Helper" (John 15:26 esv) He would send would be with us all the time.

Jesus has given you "grace to go" for every situation and to overcome every challenge. Maybe you've had glimpses of something much bigger, better, and higher for your life. Maybe, when you've let yourself dream God-dreams, you've seen things that seemed completely impossible. In those moments, there is a good chance that you responded like Moses did when God gave him his big assignment. He said, "I can't. I can't take steps in that direction. I can't go!" But God's grace turned Moses' "I can'ts" into "I cans." I want you to discover the same can be true for you. With grace—supernatural empowerment from Heaven—you can turn your personal *I can'ts* into *I cans* as well.

....

Motion activates God's power in our lives.

....

God loves progress. He wants us to grow and develop in ways that make us more resiliant and stronger and have greater faith. It doesn't mean we won't face challenges. It means that we will have more faith in Him so we can get through those challenges. He's the God of "Get Unstuck." The God of "Climb Out of Your Rut." The God of "Move Forward." Motion activates God's power in our lives. I'm here to encourage you that the only way to grow is to go. The only way to expand your territory is to push past what's holding you back. You have to get moving to find your promised land.

My heart for this book—my hope for you—is that you will discover all the gifts, talent, and courage God placed inside of you, and understand that it's never too late. Regardless of the season of life you're in or what past disappointments and setbacks you've experienced, you are graced to go. You can have that life you've dreamed of.

I write this to inspire you to go. To get moving. You still have a big, beautiful life to live. I have a friend who says, "You don't steer a car unless it's moving." God wants to steer us in the direction of all the favor and blessing He has for us, but we must get going. We can't do that if we are frozen in fear, discouragement, or insecurity. Again: Motion activates God's power in our lives.

If you can move into something comfortably and in your own strength, not much faith is required. It is only when you're uncomfortable or beyond what you think you can accomplish that it is necessary to stretch your faith and partner with God. It's only when you feel over your head, out of your depth, and unsure of your own ability that you know you've stepped onto the path toward God's highest and best. That's when you will see things happen you couldn't make happen on your own.

That's why He's always pulling us out of our comfort zones and into something that's bigger than we think we can do. You're about to discover that you are far more capable than you know. And when grace adds God's *super*natural to your natural ability, that's when miracles happen.

That grace to go is fully available to us as children of God. But we have to be open to receiving it. And receiving requires faith. So up ahead you'll find keys to receiving grace to go and a lot of inspiring stories that will stir your faith. As you read them, please keep in mind, God loves you and if He did it for them, He will do it for you.

Here's what I so want you to know down in your deepest "knower." God made you in His extraordinary image. He calls you a masterpiece. He's equipped you. And He will empower you. I hope to convince you that you are not lacking anything necessary to fulfill your highest, most fulfilling destiny. That you're not at a disadvantage. On the contrary, with God *in* you, *for* you, and *behind* you, you're advantaged in every way.

I have a heart to see you live that bigger, better adventure, and I've poured that heart out onto these pages. I hope to help you see things in yourself that you currently can't see. To build in you confidence that—no matter what season of life you're in, no matter what disappointments or setbacks you've experienced in the past—you *still* can have that life.

You may not feel *any* of that today. As I've discovered on my own journey, this is what faith is all about. I hope to plant and nourish the seeds of that kind of faith in you as we go along. That's why you'll find "Grace Thoughts" and "Grace Reflections" at the end of each chapter. I hope you'll water those seeds yourself by speaking them out loud, boldly and often.

More than anything else, I hope you'll discover that when you just GO with what you have, you'll soon find that you have even more than you know.

Are you ready? Let's *go!*

GRACED TO GO

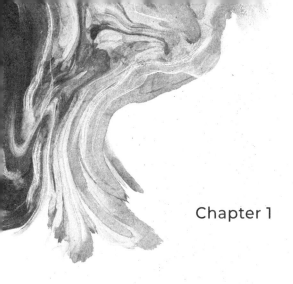

Chapter 1

GO IN THE STRENGTH YOU HAVE

Have you ever felt stuck? Maybe a change that you wanted to make, a goal you wanted to reach. Or maybe you encountered an unusually challenging situation that you were determined to face head-on. You started out strong but because of roadblocks or unfortunate circumstances, you lost sight of what could be. Now the dream looks too big, the problem too great. You tried, but it didn't work out. Now it seems like it's too late.

At times we all experience unfamiliar circumstances or transitions in our lives that make us feel uneasy and even fearful. We don't feel qualified. We don't have the training, the connections, or the experience for what's in front of us. Any time you try to move forward, voices whisper, "You're not strong enough, good enough, talented enough."

It's easy to let self-doubt, insecurity, or fear keep us from stepping into the new things God has in store for us. The defeating thoughts and feelings come swiftly and noisily, threatening to drown out God's reassuring and affirming voice, pulling us away from the vision, the dream, the calling. How do we stand firm in the knowledge that we wouldn't be facing the giant if God hadn't already given us a sling? How do we trust the promise that with God's blessing and favor, we will bring down giants?

How can we live our days in the knowledge that we are not lacking, not at a disadvantage, not too old or too young, that we have everything we need to fulfill the destiny that God has appointed for us?

Moving into God's promises requires faith in action. It's about getting out of the comfort and confines of what you think you are capable of and trusting that God can lead you into the places He has for you. For most of us, that means reaching for more than what we think is attainable.

It means stepping across the line that fear has drawn. It means being willing to take on projects and responsibilities that may look overwhelming to you. It's understanding that God has allowed that challenge in your life because He knows you're capable of overcoming it.

It's tempting to shrink back, but when you listen, you'll hear that still small voice telling you to move forward. When you take that step of faith, God will step in and help you do what you feel you can't do. You'll discover ability that you didn't know you had.

You can't wait until your fear disappears. You may have to step out in faith, in spite of the fear. You may never feel like all the conditions are right. Too many of us are living with hidden dreams, unused talents, and untapped potential simply because we've let fear convince us to play it safe.

....

**You can't wait until your fear disappears.
You may have to step out in faith,
in spite of the fear.**

....

I've written this book to help you take that step of faith, to live actively within the belief that God has equipped you to do what He has called you to. No one who's ever done anything great in life has done it without fear. So let's learn how we're graced to go—not in the strength we *wish* we had—but in the strength we do have, through God's infinite power, His love for us, and through the amazing plans He has for each of our lives.

SMALL IN YOUR OWN EYES

In the Scripture, Saul was handpicked by God to be the first king of Israel. He played a crucial role in uniting the Israelites under one leadership toward the end of the period of "the Judges."

There was much to admire about Saul, the man God told the prophet Samuel to anoint as the king. The Scripture says that he was tall and handsome, gifted in leadership. But when it was time for Saul to be crowned king in front of the people, they couldn't find him.

Eventually, someone found him hiding among the bundles and boxes where the supplies were kept. Even though he had a powerful experience with God, and had already been anointed for the job, he hid from his calling because he didn't see himself the same way God saw him. He was fearful to accept the challenge placed before him and he risked not becoming all God called him to be. Ultimately, Saul did rise to the occasion and, years later, the prophet Samuel referred to that moment when He asked Saul, "Although you were once small in your own eyes, did you not become the head of the tribes of Israel?" (1 Samuel 15:17).

Saul was not the only person chosen and called by God for great things who chose to hide because they were "small in their own eyes." Many of us have done the same thing for the same reason.

MY FIRST TRIP OUT OF
THE COMFORT ZONE

When I was thirteen years old, with all the insecurities and self-doubts that usually come with that age in life, my mother wanted me to work with her on the weekends at our family's jewelry store. It wasn't as if the store and its ways were unfamiliar to me. As a child, I'd spent countless hours watching her and other employees on the sales floor. But the idea of answering customers' questions about fine jewelry at that age was way out of my comfort zone. My mother lovingly encouraged me, saying she understood my fears and insecurities, but she was certain I had the gifts and talents I needed.

Nevertheless, I remember the knot in my stomach every time the moment came to step out of the back room and onto the sales floor. Usually, after all the jewelry was put into the display cases, I would head straight for the safety of the back room. I found every reason to stay busy in the back. It was only when there were too many customers in the store and the sales staff was fully occupied that I was forced to come out.

My mother knew I had what it took to succeed. But she also knew that I would have to move forward if that success was going to be achieved. Although I didn't see myself as capable at first, and I surely didn't feel that way, she continued to teach me and train me in the business. In so many ways I didn't always feel comfortable. It was stretching me, but as I gained more confidence, the fear and insecurity lost its strength. In time, I grew to enjoy working with the customers.

Sure, it was frightening at first, and I was unsure of myself, but my mother was there to train me, and I slowly learned the business. My confidence grew once I got moving. When I started seeing myself the right way, not only did I survive in this new role, I thrived. As time went on, I became the top salesperson in my mother's company. Before long, I had regular customers whose trust and loyalty I had earned and who specifically requested my help when they came in. Taking that first, scary step took me on a literal journey around the world as a buyer and designer of fine jewelry.

Here's the thing…all of that potential success, accomplishment, growth, and adventure was in me all along. God had already graced me to go. But I could have let fear of failure, concern about what people were going to think, or how I saw myself, keep it from coming out. Those insecurities and self-doubt could have kept me from growing and experiencing the new things that God wanted to show me.

God is a transformational God. He always leads us one step at a time. My time of learning at my mother's store helped me develop skills and gain experiences I never would have discovered if I had said, "This is not for me. Too uncomfortable. I would rather stay behind the scenes and play it safe."

So many good things came from my time at my mother's jewelry store. I met the love of my life there when Joel came into that very same store one day to buy a watch battery. When I think back on all of my experiences and challenges, I can see how each step God has asked me to take created and prepared me for other moments of destiny that would come further down the road.

I am so thankful that my wise mother knew then what I only discovered later—that God never meant for us to live little lives. That there is always more in us than we know or perceive in the present moment.

"THE LORD IS WITH YOU, MIGHTY WARRIOR"

In Judges 6, we find God's people, the Israelites, being continually raided, robbed, and oppressed by powerful tribes of desert nomads called the Midianites and Amalekites. During this turbulent period of the judges, with no formal government or army, the twelve tribes of Israel were basically powerless to stop the raiders from the wilderness who came "like swarms of locusts and whose numbers were impossible to count."

Because of the incessant raids on their fields and livestock, the Israelites lost their confidence that their God would fight their battles for them and were living their lives just hoping to avoid the thieves. It's no surprise then for us to find a future warrior, Gideon, safely steering clear of the raiders by holing up in a winepress, threshing wheat. That's right: The story of a man we now know as one of the great, heroic military leaders of the Bible begins with him essentially hiding, hoping to protect himself, with no inkling of his destiny. Certainly, the thought of being a hero to his people never occurred to him.

But God had bigger and better plans for Gideon, and it started with helping him see himself as God saw him. When he was in the winepress threshing wheat, an angel of the Lord appeared and said, "The Lord is with you, mighty warrior" (Judges 6:12). Those words must surely have changed the atmosphere in that winepress. It challenged Gideon's attitude and perspective about two things: himself and his circumstances. But Gideon's response was one of complete confusion. There was nothing about the angel's greeting that made any sense to him at that moment.

Rather than pause and let God's Word sink into his spirit, Gideon did what we often do. We hear our Heavenly Father greeting us with declarations in His Word of who we really are: "Victorious. Capable. Valuable. Strong. Masterpiece. Highly favored." We question it. We think, "You can't be talking about *me*."

As we often do, Gideon questioned the good news. Upon hearing the angel's greeting, he replied with a skeptical question. He basically asked the angel, "If that is the case, where is the God who worked wonders in the past, bringing the Israelites out of Egypt?" It's clear that Gideon was not only fearful, but he was discouraged and bitter about the long, humiliating defeat his people labored under. He and his people had been mistreated and taken advantage of for so long that it looked hopeless. He was saying, "God, where have You been?"

I love the Lord's messenger's response to Gideon. Rather than dwell on the past, he said, "Gideon, go in the strength you have and save Israel out of Midian's hand. Am I not sending you?" God was saying, "You go, Gideon. Go in the strength you have. Not the strength you *wish* you had. Not in the strength some other person who you think is more qualified has. I will be with you. Go confidently, knowing that I, the Almighty God, am sending you."

God didn't say, "Gideon, stay where you are until you get some leadership classes." He didn't say, "Don't move until you understand it or feel totally equipped." He didn't say, "Wait until things change and are looking favorable." No, God said, "Go! Go, and, as you get moving, I'll give you more strength along with whatever else you need to have victory. I will be with you. I'll give you grace to go and succeed."

When you use what you have—no matter how little it

seems—God will multiply it. Don't wait until you feel like a mighty hero. God works in our circumstances when we have faith, even the smallest amount of it. God's promises are motion-activated.

....

> God works in our circumstances
> when we have faith, even
> the smallest amount of it.

....

However, Gideon wasn't convinced by God's "Go." He still had questions. "Pardon me, but how can I save Israel? My clan is the weakest in Manasseh, and I am the least in my family" (Judges 6:15).

Gideon was saying: "You have the wrong guy, Lord. My family lacks in so many areas, and I surely don't have what it takes. Obviously, You haven't realized that we can never seem to get ahead."

He was certain he had a rock-solid excuse for why he was unqualified for this divine assignment. It was interesting how God was not seeing him the way he saw himself. What a contrast in the two perspectives. While Gideon's mind was focused only on the problems he was facing, and how he was going to survive, God had bigger and higher thoughts about him. He was looking at Gideon's future, and what he could become. Gideon saw himself as weak, not able, but God saw a fearless, courageous warrior.

Gideon's self-image was out of sync with God's view. Could it be that your self-image is also out of sync with God's true vision of who you are? Unqualified, weak, or insignificant for what God is asking you to do and be? We all have negative thoughts that push us back and try to talk us out of what is in our hearts, thoughts that may come from past failures or from voices from our pasts that told us we don't have what it takes.

God calls you His masterpiece. There is power in dwelling on this truth, letting it drop into your spirit, and repeating it to yourself over and over. You are a highly favored son or daughter of the Most High God, and it's important to declare over yourself what He says about you. When you echo back God's thoughts toward you, it will change the atmosphere in your winepress. It will set you up with the strength to do what God has destined you to do.

He's saying, "I am with you. I am for you. I have an amazing destiny waiting for you. So…Go! Stop sitting in the winepress waiting until you have what you think is enough. Go in whatever strength and ability you currently have now. I will give you all the grace you will ever need."

LOSE THE WAIT

In order to see God go to work, Gideon had to step over the line of fear and get out of the winepress. He had to decide to trust God and take the bold step God had asked him to take. He had to do some things that were surely uncomfortable for him. He had to lose the wait and be obedient to the go. It's in the obedience that brings the strength. The same is true for you and me. With faith and trust, we have to do whatever it is God is asking us to do. The moment we start moving in that direction, we find ourselves receiving all the strength we need. We find that God is with us. We must learn that fear is a feeling, and we can overcome fear through making the decision to trust and obey what God is asking us to do. That's where faith comes in. Faith should activate our actions.

It is so easy to get stuck waiting. Waiting for people to believe in us. Waiting until we get to a place of strength. Waiting to feel more qualified. Waiting for the economy to improve. Waiting for just the right circumstances. We have to *lose the wait*. Start moving in the direction of your

God-given dreams and desires. It's the only way to see brighter days.

Several years ago, during one spring break, I took my daughter, Alexandra, and my niece Elizabeth to a hotel on the coast. I thought an all-girls' spring break retreat would not only be fun, but it would give me a perfect opportunity to connect more deeply with my fourteen-year-old daughter. Of course, my daughter and niece had different priorities. They were more concerned with getting beach time than anything else, and it was their shared goal to return to school perfectly tanned. Not my first goal, but I was good with it. So off we went in search of sunshine.

The entire first day we were greeted by gray skies wrapped in fog. We sat around the hotel and only went outside to eat lunch by the shady pool. The second day the conditions were the same. After two sunless days, the girls were frustrated and complaining. On day three, the girls were so desperate they went to the beach anyway, lying out in the middle of gray gloom and fog. It was a sad sight. At dinner that night, they were so disappointed that they didn't even plan to put on their bathing suits the next day.

As expected, the weather the next day was just more of the same. Hoping to salvage what was left of their spring break, I said, "It's time for a change of scenery," so we decided to drive into the city and have lunch. Unexpectedly, the closer we got to the city, the brighter everything around us was. It didn't take us long to realize that not far from our hotel, just a mile or so down the road, the sun had been shining the whole time.

The sky was a glorious blue, the sun was shining, and the girls' moods lifted instantly. As it turned out, our hotel had been under a "marine layer" of clouds and fog. We just had to move a short distance to enjoy spectacular weather.

Many times it's the same way in life. We look around and just see fog, gloom, or discouraging circumstances. Thoughts whisper, "It's permanent. You'll never get well. Never meet the right person. Never get the breaks to accomplish the dream." But what we can't see is it's just a season. Just a little further, there are sunny skies. Favor, good breaks, the right people, new opportunities. Don't let the fog fool you. Don't let the dark clouds convince you to stay where you are. Take some steps of faith. Go a little further, try another option, do something you haven't done. That fog you're under may not move just yet, but it's not everywhere. When you go in the strength you have, you'll discover the brighter days that will move you into your destiny.

I once talked with a woman who was overwhelmed by depression after her husband left her unexpectedly. She thought her life was doomed. She had no vision for her future. All she felt was a heartache and pain, and she was paralyzed by the fear of never being happy again. It felt so real that she couldn't even get out of bed. She began spending day after day in a darkened bedroom with the door shut. Friends called but they rarely got an answer. She was as stuck as anyone could imagine. Then one day, at a friend's encouragement, she made just one tiny little move. She summoned all her strength and will and... opened the curtains. That's it. Just the smallest and simplest of steps. She let the sun in.

Soon, seeing some blue sky and green leaves got her to a place where she could take a walk. A few walks led to conversations and coffee and other little joys of everyday life. She gained more strength and began to hope again. She simply started moving. A few little steps led to bigger steps and soon her smile was back. Then she got back to work, believing that life could be good again. And it was. Today she's flourishing. She has great relationships and uses her experience to always speak hope and faith into others. Things wouldn't have turned around like they did, if she hadn't used the strength she had and taken that first step.

How about you? Are you waiting to feel stronger, more prepared, or better situated before you step out? Maybe it's time to lose the wait. You need energy to be strong, and energy exists when something is moving. Simply put, you can't grow stronger until you get going.

If you feel stuck, take a step. Even the smallest step can get you moving toward a better future. Open a window. Make that phone call. Ask that question. Do that thing that seems like just a little bit of a stretch. Face that task that intimidates you a little. That's how you build your strength and confidence. That's how you start believing in yourself again. From where you stand today, each day may seem cloudy, dreary, and shrouded in fog, but I can assure you that there are clear skies and sunshine only a short distance away.

GO WITH WHAT YOU HAVE

If you read the rest of Gideon's story, you might be amazed at the steps God asks him to take. At one point, God instructs him to do something that must have perplexed him and made him feel that God was asking him to do the impossible. But Gideon chose to trust God and to overcome his own doubts. God called upon

Gideon—the least among his family—to rally the people of Israel to band together and form a fighting force to challenge the Midianite marauders. Gideon believed what God said about him and then he moved. And when he moved, he gained the energy and the anointing he needed to accomplish his task. He put aside his fears, replaced his timidity with confidence, and inspired Israelites across the land to follow him and resist those they feared most.

Gideon was a new man; faithful, passionate, and inspiring. He left the winepress and raised an army of 32,000 Israelite men—a fighting force that was fully capable of dealing with the Midianites. Now, most of us might assume that when going into battle, having more soldiers is better than fewer. But contrary to everything Gideon expected, God asked him to do something that must have seemed so odd.

God told Gideon to reduce the size of his army and He told Gideon how to do it. Gideon trusted God— against all human instincts—and did as God commanded. Gideon reduced his "army" from 32,000 fighting men to an eventual 300. Throughout the Scripture, God works through the few. He gave Gideon instructions on how to conquer with less, and Gideon obeyed. Gideon passed the test and accepted what seemed like ridiculous odds in battle, showing how his faith in God's plan and his own confidence was growing.

I love this story because it tells us so much about our wonderful God. Gideon's tiny army went up against a huge army and defeated them. How? Because, in faith, Gideon went in the strength he had. God loves to fight our battles and defeat our enemies when we trust Him and get moving. It's not about how much you have but how you use what you have. It's about how you go in the strength you have. Not only will you step up to a new level, but you'll also see God fight battles and defeat armies on your behalf. He'll give you supernatural victories. He'll open doors of opportunity you could never have opened on your own.

> It's not about how much you have
> but how you use what you have.

We also learn that when Gideon's 300 soldiers ran toward the enemy, they shouted, "For the Lord and for Gideon!" What an amazing reversal that shows. Gideon went from the isolation of fear in the winepress to having

a whole victorious army shouting his name. That's what
happens when you go in the strength you have, choose
to see yourself the right way, and trust God to give you
strength and success. You find honor. You find favor. You
find yourself standing in places you could never have
imagined.

STEPPING OVER THE FEAR LINE

In 1999, Joel's father, John Osteen, passed unexpectedly.
He and Dodie founded Lakewood. He loved to preach
and hardly ever missed preaching on Sundays. After he
passed, Joel began ministering to the congregation almost
immediately, but it was several months later before he was
officially named senior pastor. I knew that once he became
the senior pastor, I would be expected to participate in the
Sunday services in a big way. And that would include a
lot of public speaking from the platform. That was way
outside of my comfort zone.

Those few months before Joel officially assumed leadership were filled with fear as I thought about standing up
and speaking in front of thousands of people each week-
end. I didn't want to do it any more than the thirteen-year-
old me wanted to wait on customers at my mother's store.

Those same voices of fear bombarded my mind, "You won't be able to help anybody. You have nothing to say to them. You're going to be so embarrassed. You won't even be able to get words to come out of your mouth."

Several months passed and Joel was officially made senior pastor. My time had come as well, and I was still in dread. For a while, I let it make me miserable. The thought of having to stand on that platform occupied my mind all week long. All my fearful, negative thoughts were still speaking to me, and the only way I knew to silence them was to pray. I prayed for wisdom, confidence, and strength, and I prayed for God's help even though I felt over my head.

After all, I had never signed up for this, so why was I now in this position?

I had to talk myself out of making excuses for why I couldn't do this and start talking to myself about how I was going to accomplish this new assignment.

God helped me to understand that He knows what I am feeling. God knew I was married to Joel and God knew what Joel would be doing. So I had to realize that God knew what *I* would be doing. That realization set me free from the fear, dread, and crisis of confidence that was holding me captive. If God had called me to this, He would help me overcome any obstacle that would hold me back.

I set my mind on the truth: *This is God's plan, so I am placing it in God's hands.* I started seeing myself (in God) as bigger than the fear that was trying to torment me. I started saying out loud the things I knew God has spoken to me. I replaced those negative thoughts with God's thoughts toward me, such as, "God chose me. He called me, and He has equipped me. I have the strength and ability to succeed and thrive in this. I am who God says I am. I can do what God says I can do!"

That confidence didn't come instantly. It was a process that came through continuing to take steps of faith. I had to imagine myself stepping over that line of fear every time I would get up to speak. As I would walk up, I physically took a step over that perceived fear, and little by little I gained more confidence until I became bolder than the fear that was in front of me.

Stay consistent and keep pushing against the fear harder than it is pushing against you. You may not realize it, but every time you do, you're getting stronger and what's holding you back is getting weaker.

Proverbs 4:18 says, "The path of the righteous is like the morning sun, shining ever brighter till the full light of day." Think about it. Days don't go from dark night to bright light in one instant. Dawn comes gradually. But it comes. Always.

When you find yourself in a position where more is expected of you than you think you can deliver, understand this: God knows what is happening to you. He wouldn't have allowed it if you weren't well able to handle it. He knows what you are capable of even when you don't. When you feel unprepared or unqualified, keep your mind going in the right direction. Not, "This is too much; why is this happening? I'll never accomplish my dream." Turn it around: "I am well able. God has armed me with strength for this battle. His favor surrounds me like a shield." If you'll keep the right mind-set and go in the strength you have, God will turn that stumbling block into a stepping stone to take you to a new level of your destiny.

....

He wouldn't have allowed it if you
weren't well able to handle it.

....

When Joel and I married in 1987, he was the producer-editor of his father's television broadcast. He had studied film and television production in college and was perfectly content to produce Lakewood's TV broadcasts—behind the scenes and out of sight. When his father passed, Joel felt the Lord calling and urging him to step up and pastor the church but he didn't feel qualified. He had never ministered before. He didn't have the training. He could have let the voices of fear, discouragement, and self-doubt convince him to stay where it was comfortable. But he could hear the still small voice saying, "Joel, go in the strength you have and I will be with you." He made that decision to take the step of faith and he began to minister each Sunday.

I noticed Joel was wearing his father's shoes: a pair of custom-made Italian shoes we'd given his father as a special gift a few years before. Sure, it was sweetly symbolic that he was filling his father's shoes. But I believe it was more significant than that. Joel was drawing strength from those shoes. They were a reminder that his Heavenly Father was with him just as He had been with his father, and because God was with him, he had the strength he needed to take every step of the way.

Joel understood that this challenge, even though it opposed his quiet nature and inclination to remain behind the scenes. Like Gideon, God was calling him from behind the scenes into a place he could experience new levels of his destiny.

For the first eleven months in his new role, Joel wore those shoes. Then on the first Sunday of 2000, Joel put on his own shoes. For a season, he borrowed strength and confidence from what those shoes meant. Joel wasn't trying to be like or feel like his dad. Rather, those shoes were a reminder of the encouraging words his father had spoken to him and over him. A reminder of the love and strong belief in him his father had always shown. Although the transition was difficult, Joel simply had to do his part, and stepping into those shoes outwardly represented the steps of faith he was taking spiritually. It happened one faith step at a time as he trusted God to give him the strength.

In Gideon's story, we see that every time he made a move in faith, his confidence grew. The same happened with Joel. Crossing the line of fear and stepping onto that platform to speak was huge. But he did it. And little by little, he saw more strength and favor.

On the path to your destiny, there will be times you feel like you're at a disadvantage. You're outnumbered, outsized, out-trained, and out-educated. The enemy wants you to stay in fear. To stay stuck in wrong mindsets. Stuck in regret from past mistakes. Stuck in the pain of past wounds. He knows if you get moving in faith and keep taking steps, you're sure to reach the fullness of your God-given destiny. You have to understand this principle, to go in the strength you have even when you're sure it's not enough. But here is great news: God has given you all you need. Go with the strength you have, and God will do the rest.

IT'S TIME TO GET MOVING

Gideon would have never experienced his amazing future had he not changed his mind-set—that his past limited his future. In that winepress, his thoughts about the future were limited to what he had always known in the past: defeat. Gideon chose to avoid the challenge and, like a lot of us, was just making do with what little he had. What was really defeating Gideon were his thoughts. So God came to him to shift his mind-set and eliminate the thoughts that were not allowing him to see what he could become.

As He did with Gideon, sometimes God will let the odds be against you to show Himself strong on your behalf. It's all a part of His plan. Although we tend to look at the little we have as not enough, God sees it as more than enough. Using the little we have is the key that unlocks the door to what God has. We must give God something to work with. We must look beyond what we have to what God can do with our obedience. We must shift our focus off of ourselves and our inabilities and place it on His power and ability.

Like Saul, you may be little in your own eyes. Like Gideon, you may not have a clear vision of how God can use you and do great things through you. Perhaps fear and doubt have convinced you that you cannot possibly be that person and your life could never be better. Our mind-set can be enveloped in a blanket of fog so thick that the possibilities never shine through.

Here's what I want you to understand. When you make a move, God makes a move. When you decide to get out of the winepress—when you step over the line of fear—you will begin to see new possibilities. Only a mile down the road the sun is shining and the sky is blue. So lose the wait. Go with the grace you have, and you'll find out what God really wants to do in you and through you.

Gideon took a step. Now it's your turn. Do what God is impressing on your heart to do. He will use what you have, then He'll show you He has much more than you can imagine. He'll do the impossible.

Grace Thoughts

- God calls me His masterpiece. He has equipped me. And He will empower me.

- I will go in the strength I have. Not the strength I *wish* I had. God is with me.

- Sometimes, when I feel stuck, I know that just the smallest, seemingly insignificant movement can set me on the road to better days.

- Faith means trusting that God will give me the ability to do what He has asked me to do. I trust Him.

- I have a Heavenly Father who has spoken amazing and wonderful things over me. His Word is filled with promises that belong to me.

- I will step over the "fear line." I will see myself (in God) as bigger than the fear that is standing in front of me, and I am growing in confidence daily.

- I am not small in my own eyes. I see God using me to do great things.

Grace Reflections

1. In what area of my life am I being pulled out of my comfort zone?

   ....

   ....

   ....

2. Are there any areas in my life in which I am "little in my own eyes"?

   ....

   ....

   ....

3. Is there a "line of fear" I need to step over?

   ....

   ....

   ....

4. What does the next step look like?

   ....

   ....

   ....

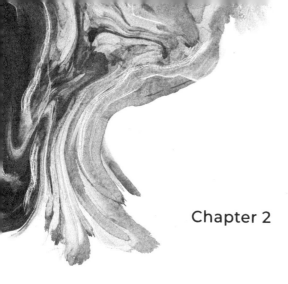

Chapter 2

GO IN THE POSITION YOU ARE IN

The Scripture talks about how God has written every day of our lives in His book. He's already lined up what we need to fulfill our purpose—the good breaks, the open doors, the right people, solutions to problems. There is an abundant, rewarding future in store for each one of us. But here's the key: God doesn't show us the whole plan. He doesn't give us all the details.

For example, He told Abraham to leave his country and go into a land that He would show him. God knew where He was taking him. He already had the location, which route to travel, how long it would take, what he would need, but He didn't tell Abraham any of that. I'm sure Abraham asked God for the details as he was contemplating making this move. "Where am I going? How far is it? What's the weather going to be like? Will there be any opposition? God, just show me, then I'll go." But God says, go and *then* I'll show you.

Like Abraham, when we feel God leading us to do something, we want to know the details. How's this going to work out? Where are the funds going to come from? Do I have the connections, the training, the experience? This is what faith is all about. You have to go, trusting that God is ordering your steps, that He has a good plan for your life, and that as you go, you'll see His plan begin to unfold.

I was walking to a department store one evening. I wasn't sure if it was still open. The doors were closed, and no one was coming in or out. Throughout the whole walk from the parking lot, my thoughts were saying, "It's too late, you might as well turn around, it's closed." As I got closer, there were still no signs of it being open. I was tempted to turn around. But when I got a few feet from the door, the doors automatically opened. I walked right in.

God works much the same way. There are doors in your life that will only open if you walk toward them. It's easy to think of all the reasons why we can't go. "I need more details, more training, a better position. God, show me a sign that it's going to work out." There may not be a sign. But when you do what God is asking you to do, you take that step of faith, at some point you'll step into that place where the door automatically opens. Don't wait for the right position, then you'll go. Don't wait until you have all the details, you feel qualified, you have the training. You have to go in the position that you're in, and then you'll see the hand of God doing what only He can do.

MORE THAN A QUEEN—A HERO

There was a beautiful young Jewish girl in the Scripture named Esther. She was an orphan living in Persia under the protection of her older cousin Mordecai among the Jews who had been carried into exile from Jerusalem by Nebuchadnezzar, king of Babylon. Growing up among the persecuted minority group, she must have felt terribly alone and forsaken and at a disadvantage, and there was no reason to think that she would ever do anything great. But when Xerxes, the Persian king, did a nationwide search for a new queen, God caused Esther to stand out, and she soon found herself on the threshold of becoming queen of the most powerful empire on the face of the Earth at that time.

Esther was understandably nervous about stepping through this improbable, open door. She had never dreamed of becoming a queen. There was nothing in her background that had prepared her for this moment. But she sensed the favor of God was on her life, and she felt the courage to dare to step out of the obscure position she had been in. Out of all the beautiful women in the empire, Xerxes chose her over others who came from wealth and influence. God took Esther from the background to the front.

That, however, was only the beginning. There was a powerful court official named Haman who came to so hate Mordecai that he convinced the king to sign a decree to kill all the Jewish people in the empire. Mordecai, who had forbidden Esther to reveal her nationality, told her she had to go into the king's inner court and plead with Xerxes to spare her people. But the law stated that if anyone approached the king without being summoned, they would be put to death unless he held out the gold scepter. When she expressed her reservations and fears to Mordecai, he gave his famous reply:

> "...Who knows if you may have attained royal position for such a time as this?" (Esther 4:14 MEV)

You've surely heard the phrase "...for such a time as this." What kind of time was it for Esther? A time in which all the Jewish people were in danger of being victims of a genocide. God was asking her to step into the unknown and put her life on the line for her people.

I love that Esther stepped up and said, "I will go to the king, even though it is against the law. And if I perish, I perish" (Esther 4:16). In today's language, she was saying, "I'm all in." In church circles we might say, "I'm climbing out of the boat," referring to Peter stepping out to walk on water with Jesus in the middle of a raging storm.

It's like Moses heading back to Egypt to face Pharaoh, the most powerful man in the world, to deliver a message from God he knew Pharaoh wouldn't like. Esther's brave declaration is a lot like those three Hebrew boys living in Babylon facing a terrible death for refusing to bow down to pagan idols, saying, "If we are thrown into the blazing furnace, the God we serve is able to deliver us from it, and he will deliver us from Your Majesty's hand. But even if he does not, we want you to know, Your Majesty, that we will not serve your gods or worship the image of gold you have set up" (Daniel 3:17–18).

In the face of fear, Esther found the courage and faith to be obedient, stepping into her destiny and saving her people.

Friend, you, too, were born for such a time as this. God could have placed you in any era of history and in any place. But you are here, where you are, for reasons born in the heart of God Himself.

Esther had plenty of excuses for staying invisible among the thousands of young Jewish women living in the Persian Empire. She was the "wrong" race. Belonged to the "wrong" religion. And the personal dangers involved in interceding with the king on behalf of her people were very real.

It would have been so easy to just stay put. To stay hidden. But Esther chose to "go." To go in the position she was in. When she stepped out, God's grace and favor opened doors for her. That favor made her a queen. And with a heart to risk her own life to save her people, she became their hero and still inspires us today.

There will be times God will ask you to do things that you don't feel qualified for. You don't have the experience. The task is too big. When you look at where you are and consider the obstacles, you'll be tempted to shrink back, listen to all the thoughts telling you how you're at a disadvantage, you don't have what you need. But like Esther, if you'll go from where you are, knowing that God is with you, His favor will begin to make things happen you couldn't make happen. You'll discover ability you didn't know you had, the courage and strength to accomplish more than you thought possible.

....

Dare to take steps of faith.
The hero in you is waiting to come out.

....

It's interesting that Esther was chosen as queen but history remembers her as a hero. You may never be in a palace with a crown on your head. But there are people who need you to rise up to your potential. Your family. Your children. Your community.

You can be the hero they need. You already have what it takes. You were placed where you are for such a time as this. You are graced to go. Be bold. Be confident. Dare to take steps of faith. The hero in you is waiting to come out.

A friend of mine grew up in a small town in Kentucky. His family had limited resources and struggled to make ends meet. As a little boy, even though he didn't have much, he always had a big heart of compassion, wanting to help others. One day he saw an ad on television how you could support a hungry child in another country for fifteen dollars a month. He was so moved seeing other children in need. It stirred his heart to help. He wasn't raised in a religious home. But every night before he'd go to bed, he'd say, "God, please send some wealthy person to help these children in need." He didn't have any money, but at eight years old he started mowing lawns in the neighborhood to raise the funds.

Year after year, he faithfully supported a child. By the grace of God, he was able to go to college. Eventually he was accepted into medical school. During the summers, instead of taking time off, he would go on medical mission trips with a group of doctors to treat children with dysentery, parasites, malaria, and other diseases from unsanitary conditions. After graduation, he became very successful in his medical practice, specializing in internal medicine and infectious disease.

In spite of all the demands for his time and expertise, he continued to use his vacations to travel overseas and treat needy children. One of his medical suppliers heard about it, and they started donating medicines, vaccines, and antibiotics. A shoe company donated a hundred thousand shoes to him. The donations got so large, he had to rent a warehouse to hold it all. Today our friends, Dr. Todd and Sue Price, have donated over a billion dollars in supplies and medicines to children around the world. Todd always thought that God would send a wealthy person to help the children. After his organization had treated over twenty million children, he said, "I realized God had answered my prayer, but not like I thought. *I was the person I was praying for.*" He was looking for someone else, but the hero was in him. He thought he was at a disadvantage, with a lack of resources, from a low-income family. He never saw himself being in a position to make much of a difference. But Dr. Price did what Esther did, and what we all must do: He went from the position he was in.

Had he focused on what he didn't have and how he was lacking and how big the need was, he would have never taken the first step and started mowing the lawns. He would have never seen the favor, blessing, and goodness of God in his life to be that hero and bless so many others.

Who knows what God is going to do in your life if you'll simply go from the position you're in? This is what requires faith. Often God will put us in circumstances where we are in over our head, where the task is too big, where we're looking for the hero to step up. We don't realize we are the hero. God has called you to make a difference, to set new standards, to bless your community and the world around you. There are things He's destined you to accomplish that are bigger than you can imagine. But the question is: Will you go from the position that you're in? Will you start with what you have right now?

Don't discount where you are and what you have. It's not a surprise to God. If you'll use what you have, God will breathe on it and things will begin to increase. Dr. Price was faithful with one child, mowing lawns week after week. That was a seed that God could use to trust him with more. When you're faithful with what you have, being your best each day, taking steps of faith, it may seem small, like it's not making much difference, but your time is coming. God knows how to take little and turn it into much.

STARTING WITH A STICK, NOT A SCEPTER

Moses is one of the key figures in the Bible. God used him to do things that changed the whole course of history—not just for Israel but for the world. His call was to be one of the great heroes of the Bible. But to fulfill that destiny he had to be willing to "go from the position he was in." What was that position?

He was a herder of sheep and goats out in the middle of nowhere. And they weren't even his animals. They belonged to his father-in-law, Jethro. His only asset was his shepherd's staff—basically a long stick. That doesn't sound like a promising résumé for someone who is about to challenge one of the most powerful rulers in the world (Egypt's Pharaoh) on behalf of a whole nation of oppressed people.

When God called out to him from a burning bush, Moses had a long list of reasons why God had picked the wrong man. Here's how the Bible records that conversation:

[God said] "So now, go. I am sending you to Pharaoh to bring my people the Israelites out of Egypt."

But Moses said to God, "Who am I that I should go to Pharaoh and bring the Israelites out of Egypt?"

And God said, "I will be with you." (Exodus 3:10–12)

Notice first, God tells Moses to "go…" To get moving, "now." Then God reveals Moses' amazing future to him. An assignment that involved leading God's people out of bondage in Egypt. And Moses' response to that startling news was, "Who am I…?"

That's the same type of question we often ask when God puts dreams and promises in our hearts that seem over our head. We get a glimpse of the amazing destinies and plans He has for us and, if we're not careful, immediately disqualify ourselves.

It's interesting how God responded to Moses. He didn't fault him or condemn him for not thinking he could do it. He simply said, "I will be with you."

That's what God is saying to you. "You're not going into this alone. I will be with you every step of the way." The Creator of the universe is going before you, making crooked places straight, empowering you, and fighting your battles. You and God are a majority. When you recognize who's with you, you'll have a boldness and confidence to do what you've been called to do.

Moses went to Pharaoh and declared what God had said, to let the people go. Pharaoh was stubborn, but Moses continued to do what God instructed. After a series of supernatural events, Pharaoh agreed to let the people go. They were delivered from 430 years of oppression. They found themselves headed toward the Promised Land, a day that they had always dreamed of.

USE WHAT YOU HAVE

Moses had grown up in the palaces of Egypt. He saw how Pharaoh carried a scepter made of precious metals and encrusted with jewels. This scepter represented his authority and gave him dominion over the people and land. When he held up his scepter, there was respect and honor. On the other hand, all Moses carried was a stick. It wasn't fancy. It was an ordinary walking stick, useful for prodding wandering sheep and goats. He had no authority, no power. No one looked up to him. Who was he to talk to the leader of a country?

It's easy to discount what we have and think, "That's not enough. I don't have the position, the talent, the experience." But when you use what you have, God will breathe on it, and it will become more than enough.

As Moses led the twelve tribes of Israel—a huge multitude of people—out of the enemy's grasp, they came to the Red Sea. Looking back, they saw that Pharaoh had changed his mind about letting God's people go. Chariots and soldiers of Egypt's powerful army were heading toward them. They were trapped. The Red Sea sat like a barrier in front of them, and an enemy army sent to destroy them was closing in behind them.

I am sure Moses thought they were finished. I imagine he pleaded with God to send fire from Heaven to destroy that army. He knew if God didn't do something big and fast, it was over for all of them. In other words, Moses was looking for the spectacular to happen. He expected a major deliverance to come through an extraordinary method. But God loves to use the ordinary. In this case, He chose to use a walking stick, simply raised up toward Heaven. Neither the tool nor the way it was used was at all spectacular, but the results certainly were.

> The waters were divided, and the Israelites went through the sea on dry ground, with a wall of water on their right and on their left. (Exodus 14:21–22)

ARE YOU READY TO BE A HERO?

Moses went from the position he was in, and with what he had. Could it be that you, too, have something already in your hand that God wants to use to open supernatural doors in your life and in the lives of people around you?

That "something" may not seem like much to you. But when you make it available to God, it becomes capable of doing wondrous things. It can make you someone else's hero.

All David had was a sling. That was no match for the sword and shield and full set of armor that Goliath had. But a sling with the favor of God will bring down giants. You will defeat greater enemies with lesser equipment if you'll simply use whatever you have.

What if we, when faced with something that looks impossible, asked God to show us the opportunity in the middle of the obstacle? Esther did—and went from orphan to queen to hero. In faith and trust she chose to go from the position she was in and ultimately found herself raised up to a position of influence and power she couldn't have dreamed of. Dr Price did. Today he's impacting millions of children, something greater than he ever imagined.

Who knows what God will do with you if you'll simply go in the position you're in? Start where you are. You are not at a disadvantage. Your past has not defined you; it has qualified you. God doesn't waste anything that you've been through. It's prepared you for the amazing future God has in store.

....

Your past has not defined you;
it has qualified you.

....

WHY NOT *LEAD* FROM
THE POSITION YOU ARE IN?

"But I'm not a boss," you might be thinking. "I'm not in management. I have an ordinary position." Then lead *up*! Leading is just another word for influence. You don't have to have a title to influence others. Be the neck that turns the head. Become comfortable in your own skin and show interest in others. You'll soon find that you have influence and impact everywhere you go.

As Gideon discovered in the previous chapter, God doesn't look at outward appearances. He doesn't measure status and importance like the world does. God sees hearts.

Even when he was hiding out in the winepress, God saw Gideon's heart position. He saw a heart willing to respond and obey. Sure, Gideon questioned the assignment, but he still obeyed. Yes, he occasionally needed reassurance and confirmation, but our gracious Heavenly Father was more than happy to provide it.

Hiding in the winepress was Gideon's outward position. But his inward position was having a heart to trust God, and *that* was the position God saw. The same is true for you. Don't let people judge you by outward things because God sees you inwardly. Don't be moved by your earthly position. Instead, understand your heavenly position.

....

> Don't be moved by your earthly
> position. Instead, understand
> your heavenly position.

....

So many of the great heroes of the Bible started in small, humble circumstances. Esther, living life in a foreign land as a persecuted minority. Moses tending Jethro's sheep and goats. David doing the same thing for his father's flocks. Not only did God see in them a heart to trust and obey, but they were also faithful in the small things when no one was watching or applauding.

There is a lesson for you and me in that. We need to be the best we can be where we are, passing the heart-test of faithfulness. Then when we sense God telling us to go, we, in faith, can believe we have all that we need.

That's how faith works. You have to believe it before you see it. Faith leads you to action. The Scripture puts faith and action together. Action naturally follows real faith. And here's great news: You can *build* your faith. How? By meditating on God's promises and upon His goodness and faithfulness to you.

Friend, you are called and destined to be someone's hero. But you have to step out to discover what God has for you. What would Esther have missed if she had not been willing to risk getting out of her comfort zone and taking the courageous step into the unknown?

Go because "God is with you!" just as He told Moses. Jesus said in Matthew 28:20, "Surely I am with you always, to the very end of the age." By the way, Jesus started that conversation with His disciples by telling them to "Go...":

Then Jesus came to them and said, "All authority in heaven and on earth has been given to me. **Therefore go...**" (Matthew 28:18–19a)

Go in the position you are in. My father-in-law, John Osteen, used to say, "When you make a move, God makes a move."

You are graced to go. God will be with you every step of the way. You're ready. You're qualified. You're enough.

Grace Thoughts

+ I was born for such a time as this. I am here, where I am, for reasons born in the heart of God Himself.

+ The God of the universe says to me, "You're not stepping into this alone, My child. I will be with you every step of the way." That is more than enough for me.

+ When faced with something that looks impossible, I ask God to show me the opportunity in the middle of the obstacle.

+ I am called and destined to be someone's hero. So I will boldly step out to discover what God has for me.

+ I know God will be faithful to prepare me for the amazing positions He has planned for me, if only I am willing to trust Him enough to go from the position I'm in.

Grace Reflections

1. Esther had plenty of excuses for staying invisible among the thousands of young Jewish women living in the Persian Empire. What are my reasons for wanting to stay invisible?

   ....

   ....

2. What do I sense God asking me to do that I don't feel qualified for?

   ....

   ....

3. Moses started with a stick, not a scepter. Is what is in my hand enough?

   ....

   ....

4. Who can I be a hero to today?

   ....

   ....

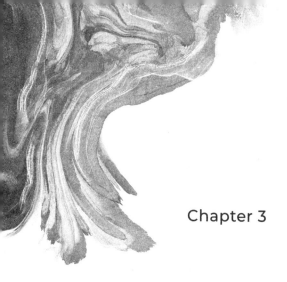

Chapter 3

GO KNOWING
YOU MATTER

It's called the "Butterfly Effect." Maybe you've heard of it. It's a concept that has been mentioned and popularized in a number of movies over the last couple of decades.

In simple terms, it's the understanding that a small action can produce big effects. The classic example is of a butterfly flapping its wings in Brazil eventually producing a tornado in Texas. It sounds ridiculous but scientists and mathematicians found this theory to be in fact viable. The butterfly effect has been widely adopted by culture and is a metaphor interpreted to mean that small events have a ripple effect that cause much larger events to occur.

God has known about the butterfly effect all along. The truth is, He invented it. So how does that apply to you and me?

With eight billion people on the planet, it can seem as if one life couldn't possibly make that much of an impact. You may be tempted to think, "Can I really make a difference just raising my children, going to work, doing my best with what I have?" Yes! Just like the butterfly effect, everything you do matters. It may feel ordinary, but it is creating extraordinary results.

Every smile, every kind word, every time you go out of your way to be good to someone, the sacrifices, staying up late, caring for that loved one, the generosity. It's all affecting not just what you can see, but even generations to come. You may never know the winds of change and all the good that will happen because of your small acts of kindness and faithfulness.

There is an unseen, unnamed woman hiding in the background of a well-known Bible story in Matthew chapter fourteen. This amazing mother likely had no idea how much she mattered and how God was going to use something ordinary and routine to impact so many others.

....

You may never know the winds of change and all the good that will happen because of your small acts of kindness and faithfulness.

....

LUNCH PAIL MIRACLES

It was just another morning. She woke up and started her day. Her to-do list was as long as usual. But first things first. She had to make lunch for her young son. This particular morning she only had two small fish left over from dinner the night before, but she did have five pieces of bread. As she began packing his lunch, doing what she always did, she never imagined what would happen later that day.

There was a huge crowd of people listening to Jesus teach. It was late in the day, and the disciples suggested dismissing the people so they could go find food. But Jesus said, "You feed them." They looked at Him, puzzled, and said, "That's impossible. We could never feed this many people." Jesus asked, "What do you have?"

After searching the crowd, all they came up with was the little boy's lunch. Five loaves and two fish. They gave it to Jesus, He blessed the food, and it multiplied. It ended up feeding over five thousand people with twelve baskets left over.

We hear a lot about the miracle of multiplying the food, but think about where it all started. A mother, being faithful. She thought it was just another routine day, checking off her to-do list, but it was a part of a bigger plan, something she couldn't see right then, a divinely orchestrated moment that years later would still be inspiring us.

That's the butterfly effect. The relationship between small movements and big events.

This mother's ordinary sandwich-making skills created an extraordinary effect. She was fluttering her wings, doing her best, and God used it. How could something as routine as taking care of your family have that kind of effect? Going to work, being your best even when you don't feel valued. Volunteering at church, helping your neighbor. It feels so normal. If this mother were here, she would tell you, "You never know the impact of your faithfulness. Keep honoring God, being good to people, going the extra mile. You're making a difference."

Think about how this mother felt when her son came flying in the door that night with the news of what happened. He probably was talking ninety miles an hour as he told her about his lunch. She thought, "You mean the five loaves, the two fish? That little lunch I made you?"

The Scripture says, "Don't despise the day of small beginnings." God loves to take our small and do big things. He'll use what we consider insignificant, or maybe ordinary, to have a tremendous impact: the little boy's lunch. Think about David's sling that he used to defeat Goliath. Moses' rod that he held up in obedience and God parted the Red Sea. Or how about Ruth's faithfulness, taking care of her mother-in-law, gathering up the leftover wheat. She never dreamed she'd meet Boaz and become the great-grandmother of King David. There's the butterfly effect. They were part of a bigger plan.

All those times you go the extra mile, give and serve, using what you have, can seem ordinary. But you don't know what God is up to. You're a part of something bigger than you can see right now. Your steps are being ordered. God has these destiny moments, like Ruth, like David, like the mother that made the lunch, where you will see what He has purposed come together.

....

**You don't know what God is up to.
You're a part of something bigger than
you can see right now.**

....

Favor, the right people, the open doors. It will seem like it happened suddenly, but the fact is, it's all those days of being faithful in the ordinary, being your best in the routine, doing the right thing when it seems insignificant. You don't realize, as you keep fluttering your wings, things are happening behind the scenes. It's not always those big events, it's the small acts of obedience. Faithfulness in our everyday life is what He uses as a ripple effect.

This truth reminds me of one of my favorite ripple-effect stories. A ripple that, because you're reading these words right now, has now touched you.

CHALKBOARD WITNESS

In 1939, in a small east Texas town, a young man named Sam Martin would get to high school early each morning and write Scriptures on the chalkboard. The other students thought it was a little odd, but that didn't stop Sam. He loved sharing his faith. It became a routine part of his morning: Early to school to write a Scripture on the blackboard.

One night a student that was in Sam's class was home alone and thinking about Heaven, wondering if it was real. He randomly opened a big Bible that had sat on the coffee table for as long as he could remember. It fell open to a picture of Jesus standing at a door knocking. The caption read, "If anyone opens the door, I will come in." The teenager's heart was stirred, and he began to think about those Scriptures Sam wrote on the blackboard.

The next day, he asked Sam about what he had seen in the Bible that night and how he had felt. Sam explained to him that that was God drawing him to Himself. That Sunday, Sam took his classmate to church. And that was the day John Osteen, Joel's father, gave his life to Christ.

Think about it. If it hadn't been for Sam Martin, we may not have known of John Osteen and Joel Osteen as we do today. John and Sam remained friends and fifty years later Sam Martin wrote a book called *I Touched One, But He Touched Millions.*

That's the butterfly effect of Sam Martin's faith. Don't ever underestimate the small acts of obedience and those times you honor God even when they seem ordinary. Sam, a quiet high school kid, simply writing Scriptures on the chalkboard each morning. It couldn't have seemed like it was making much of a difference. But in God's hands it had an incredible ripple effect. That small movement made a huge impact in John Osteen's life, who made a huge impact in so many others.

I want to remind you that your life is not ordinary. It may seem at times small or routine, but in the hands of God, you are extraordinary. You are creating ripple effects all the time. You may not be in the spotlight, but you will be rewarded for every good deed, every faithful act of obedience, your generosity, the people you encourage and the kindness you show. Your deeds are seeds. They will come back to you and spill over to future generations.

When you touch one person, that is the butterfly effect. Keep fluttering because you are leaving a legacy of faith and creating an atmosphere in which God can work.

I once saw a quote from a famous television news anchor who said, "I worked all my life to become an overnight success. And it still took me by surprise."* When we read about the heroes of faith in the Bible, it's like seeing their "highlight reels." We're amazed when Moses parted the Red Sea with his staff. And how impressive it was when David killed Goliath with just a sling and a stone. But we don't know much about their ordinary days. The forty years in the wilderness. The time that was spent in the shepherds' fields. The ordinary days were far more than the miracle highlight days.

But we can't discount that time because what they did in the ordinary was changing everything. The truth is, we're going to have more ordinary days than miraculous ones. But that's okay because those ordinary days have purpose. They set the stage and send out the ripples.

A DIVINE APPOINTMENT

This is the very truth a friend of mine discovered. She thought her job of writing letters for the company she

---

* Jessica Savitch, *Anchorwoman*, Penguin Group (1983), p. 92.

worked for was mundane and unimportant. Yet she kept a good attitude and continued doing her job to the best of her ability.

One day she received a phone call from a recipient of one of those letters. He specifically asked for her because she signed her name on behalf of the organization. He told her how much he appreciated the letter and how it brightened his day, then she went on to help him with what he needed.

To my friend, it seemed like just an ordinary call, but she had just walked into the extraordinary. That gentleman worked for a medical sales company. He had no way of knowing that my friend's sister had a serious liver condition and was in desperate need of a transplant. When he found out, he told her that he knew a doctor that could help. He introduced her to a leading specialist, who was able to give her sister a lifesaving liver transplant. Being faithful in the ordinary had set her up for a divine appointment that saved her sister's life and changed their family forever.

Like my friend, keep fluttering your wings. You may know that there is more inside you, but you're stuck in the ordinary. Can I remind you? There is no ordinary in God. When you keep a good attitude in difficult times— when you're patient, even when it is taking longer than you anticipated—you're showing God that you trust Him, in the mundane and the magnificent, in the valley and on the mountaintop. You're in the preparation season; things are happening that you can't see. Stay faithful. Learn to enjoy where you are right now. God knows when you're ready for the next season.

....

There is no ordinary in God.

....

He can make things happen that we can't make happen. It's only a matter of time before you cross over from the ordinary to the extraordinary.

GENERATIONAL RIPPLES

I have such fond memories of my grandmother. She was a remarkable woman. She loved God and knew the power of prayer.

On our family visits when I was a little girl, from my window I would see her early in the morning outside in the garden, praying for her family. I can remember the smell of her homemade biscuits baking in the oven.

One of her many talents was designing clothing. She loved to make dresses for my mother. She would put unusual colors together and mixed patterns. When my mother was growing up, every Sunday she would have a new dress hanging on the back of her door to wear to church. It gave my grandmother such joy to see my mother in those dresses. I guess that's where my mother learned design and fashion.

To my grandmother those sewing projects surely seemed ordinary. Little did she realize it was planting a seed in her daughter. Years later, with that same love of design, my mother stepped out in faith and opened a fine jewelry store. She was inspired by her mother in so many ways. And I can truly say that my mother's life has been an inspiration to me. Because my grandmother did what she did with excellence, I felt the winds in my own life many years later.

As you already know, I worked in that store as I grew up, learning the business. I never dreamed one afternoon, in that very store, this tall, dark, and handsome young man would come in needing a battery for his watch. With my amazing sales ability, I ended up selling him a whole new watch. A few days later, he called me and asked me out on a date. Joel's story is that I couldn't keep my hands off of him, so we got married. The truth is, I was so fine he couldn't stand it. More ripples.

Twelve years later, Joel's father passed, and we were asked to step up to pastor the church. Today we have the honor of bringing hope to people around the world. This all goes back to my grandmother's faithfulness. That was the butterfly effect. All those mornings praying for her family, making those dresses, what she thought was ordinary, was in fact affecting future generations. She couldn't see it at the time, but God was using her as a part of a bigger plan.

Your fluttering wings are changing
the atmosphere.

Every day you stay faithful, pray for your family, invest in those you love, take time to make those dresses, or whatever seemingly insignificant thing you do for others, doing your best—sends out ripples. Yes, at times it seems routine, it may feel ordinary, but your fluttering wings are changing the atmosphere. You're making a difference. You may not see it now, but like my grandmother, you're influencing generations to come.

SERENA'S STORY

I love the story of a friend of mine who attends Lakewood Church. Back when Serena was a senior in college, there was a young man in her math class. They spoke now and then and eventually became casual friends. They would chat as they walked to the math lab together. One day, during one of those chats, she felt a nudge, an inward impression, to invite that young man to church.

She hesitated because she didn't know him that well. She didn't know what he believed or anything about his faith background. Another inner voice said, "That's going to be kind of strange...He's going to think that's too forward...He'll be offended..." On and on the reasons and excuses for NOT obeying that nudge kept coming. So she didn't. A week went by. Then two weeks. Then a month, yet she couldn't get away from that impression that she should invite her classmate to visit church. (By the way, one way you know a nudge is from God is that it won't go away. That impression, that prompting, just keeps coming back.)

That was the case with Serena. Every time she saw him, down deep, she heard that whisper, "Invite him to church." Sometimes, God will ask you to do things that are uncomfortable, where you have to stretch and take a step of faith. During the final week of school, she finally worked her nerve up and did it. She invited him to Lakewood Church. He nodded and thanked her, but Lakewood is a big place, so she never knew whether or not he had actually visited. But she felt good that she finally obeyed that still small voice.

Serena graduated a couple of weeks later and went on with her life. Two years later, she met a wonderful young man at Lakewood, they fell in love, and were married. Life was good. Of course, Lakewood became their church home.

One day, the two of them were leaving the Sunday service when she happened to see that young man from college near the back of the auditorium. He had a volunteer badge on. He was an usher! She was amazed. She said, "I can't believe you're here and that you volunteer." Her husband went over to him and gave him a big hug and said, "Hey, how you been doing?" They began to talk like they were old friends. She looked at her husband and said, "How do you know him?" Her husband said, "He's the one that invited me to Lakewood. He's the reason that I'm here."

That whole time she was hearing that whisper, "Invite him to Lakewood," she thought she was doing him a favor;

in fact, she was doing herself a favor. That gentle whisper was saying in effect, "Invite the man who will one day invite your future husband to church!"

God sees the big picture. He knows how to connect the dots in our lives. We're never going to understand in the moment how our obedience can result in God's greater plan. Any time you hear that whisper, that impression to be good to someone else, it will not only have a positive effect on them, but it will have a positive effect on you. You may have to push past fear or uncertainty and do what God is asking you to do. You may not see how it will make a difference, but every act of obedience leads to a blessing down the road.

> We're never going to understand
> in the moment how our obedience
> can result in God's greater plan.

PAID IN FULL

When I think about how a small kindness can travel for years and ultimately come back to you in a big, big way,

I'm reminded of a story I heard about a desperately poor little boy from a small town during the era of the Great Depression.

The boy's father had died in the Spanish flu pandemic, and his mother died a few years later. In the midst of some of the hardest times our country has ever seen, he was determined to go to college. Paying his own way, every dime he could muster went to books and tuition, leaving little for food.

He took to going door-to-door selling various items to try to pay his way through school. During one particularly lean month, he had one thin dime in his pocket and he hadn't eaten properly in several days. Eventually, when his hunger got bigger than his pride, he decided that the next door he came to, he was going to ask the homeowner for something to eat.

He worked up his courage, knocked on the door of the next house, and found himself face-to-face across the threshold with a beautiful young lady. She was around sixteen years old and so pretty it took his breath away. But suddenly, pride got bigger than his hunger. There was no way he was going to admit to her he hadn't eaten in days. But he didn't have to. She could see it. So she said, "Young man, you look like you're hungry. Can I get you something to eat?" "No," he stammered, "but...but I sure could use a drink of water."

She disappeared into the interior of the house and shortly returned, carrying, not a glass of water but a big glass of cold milk. He couldn't believe his good fortune. He hadn't had milk in the longest time. It tasted so good he drank it down all in one big gulp. He instantly felt refreshed and reenergized.

Deeply grateful, he reached in his pocket for his last ten cents to pay the young lady. She quickly said, "No, you don't owe me anything. My mother taught me to never accept pay for an act of kindness." So the boy thanked her sincerely and headed on down the street.

Decades later that same young lady became seriously ill. She was examined in the small local hospital in her town, but the doctors there were mystified. So they sent her away to the big city, to the leading specialist in the state, a man named Dr. Howard Kelly. When Dr. Kelly saw her chart, the name of her hometown intrigued him. It was the same town in which he'd grown up. He rushed down to her room, took one look at her, and immediately recognized her as the young lady who had been so kind to him in a hard time.

Dr. Kelly took on this case personally. He went to

great lengths to do everything he could to make sure she got well. Sure enough, four months later she had totally recovered and was ready to leave the hospital. Dr. Kelly requested that the hospital send the medical bill through him personally. It was an unusual request but they complied, and he forwarded a new version of the bill on to her.

The woman dreaded looking at the bill, knowing that four months of the best care available would probably cost more than she could pay off in a lifetime. But when she opened that bill, Dr. Kelly had written in big letters, "PAID IN FULL WITH ONE GLASS OF COLD MILK."

You simply never know what kinds of ripples your acts of kindness and generosity are sending out. Are you paying attention to what you are feeling in your spirit? When you see a coworker or a person at the grocery store, do you feel a sense of compassion? Something says, "Let them know you care, or buy those groceries for them." It's easy to ignore. You'll be tempted to reason it out. "They look like they are doing fine." "They don't need me to encourage them." Don't ignore those impressions. You don't know how powerful your acts of kindness can be. The more you obey the more impact you will have, and God will use them in bigger ways than you could ever dream possible. He will be faithful to see that they come back to you, as

Jesus said, "Pressed down, shaken together, and running over" (Luke 6:38).

....

There are miracles in your movements.

....

What you do matters. *You* matter. The hand of God is on your life. You are graced to go out and make a difference in this world. You are not just one person in a billion. You are full of purpose and destiny. You are not ordinary; you are creating the extraordinary for those around you. Keep honoring God. Keep using your gifts and talents. Keep pouring into your family, excelling in school, stepping into your dreams. There are miracles in your movements. As you continue to flutter your wings, winds of change are happening. Because of your faithfulness, you're not only going to be a great blessing, but you're also going to be blessed in great ways; and you *will* see the faithfulness of God.

Grace Thoughts

• I believe my life is important to those around me.

• When I am faithful in the routine, things are happening that I can't see right now.

• I will be faithful in the average days and God will be faithful to show me the exceptional days.

• I will use my gifts and talents to the best of my ability and inspire those around me.

• God is using my obedience to help others even when it's out of my comfort zone.

• When I am faithful in the everyday, God is preparing me for the new things He has in my life.

Grace Reflections

1. Am I willing to keep "fluttering my wings," trusting that faithfulness in little things will have major effects and impacts eventually?

2. Am I keeping my eyes open for divine appointments in seemingly routine moments?

3. Small acts of kindness can travel for years. Where can I show kindness today?

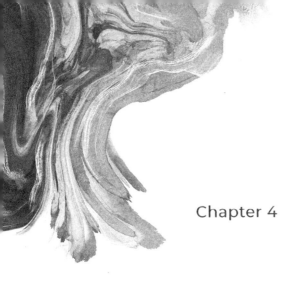

Chapter 4

GO WITH EYES
TO SEE THE GOOD

When I look back across my life, I see so many good things I learned from my mother. There are really too many to count. But one gift in particular has helped me over and over in my life.

Early on, I noticed how my mother would "reframe" difficult situations or problems or people in her life. I witnessed it every day as she ran her business. I saw her approach a grumpy customer and find the twinkle in their eyes. I watched and took note of how, whenever she had a setback, she always found a way to see the good, the bright side, or the silver lining.

But she did more than just model that. She taught it. She taught me that there was always more than one way to look at my circumstances and at the people around me. She trained me to find the good in people, even ones who may have seemed to be a problem.

This has helped me in so many areas of my life over the years. It's helped me in my relationships. It's helped me in ministry. And it's been a major key to walking through the ups and downs of life.

Difficult seasons come to everyone, me included. But that lesson learned from Mother has served me well. When I feel myself getting overwhelmed, when I'm tempted to feel negative about something hard that I'm required to do or that must be done, I have to remind myself that I have the tools to reframe those thoughts and look for the good.

When I face things that might throw me off course or stand in my way, I remember what Mother taught me— that God is *for* me, and that He is working everything for my good. Through this practice that my mother illustrated for me early on in my life, I can be "graced to go" with a new perspective that will empower me to take on the challenges in front of me and succeed.

Isn't that exactly what young David did when he faced Goliath? All the soldiers of Israel had been hiding in fear for days when David showed up. They had framed their circumstances in a negative, defensive way. And that perspective kept them stuck in defeat. David showed up and reframed the situation. He had a different mind-set. To David, there was a giant standing between him and his God-given destiny. Where his fellow Israelites saw a trained warrior way bigger than themselves, David saw someone who didn't have a covenant with the God of the universe as he did. Everyone confronted the same circumstances, but David saw them in a different way. David chose to focus on how big God was and not how big his problems were. That victory over Goliath changed the whole course of David's life and put him on a path to become the king.

As king, David had to know how to magnify the right things. He learned that if he was going to rule well, he had to view his challenges from the right perspective. He had so many chances to shrink back and see his challenges as bigger than himself, but he chose to see God as bigger than any of those things. He knew God had called him and anointed him to rule. The grace to succeed came when he made God bigger than all the hard places in his life. Is it any wonder he wrote numerous psalms that say, "Come magnify the Lord with me!"?

David knew this powerful truth: *What you magnify matters.*

....

What you magnify matters.

....

TURN YOUR TELESCOPE AROUND

When I think about magnifying the right thing, I'm reminded of a story I read years ago about a little boy and his telescope. He was ten years old and lived down the street from a bigger boy who had been bullying him. The bully made his life so miserable that he hardly dared to leave his yard. And he always took the long way home from school so he wouldn't have to pass by the other boy's house. For some time, the little boy had been trying to muster enough nerve to stand up to this mean kid, but he never did. The bully just looked so big and intimidating.

On the boy's birthday, his father bought him a

telescope he had yearned for. He was so excited. Later the father found him playing with it in the front yard and noticed that his son was looking through the wrong end, raising the larger lens to his eye. On a mission to correct him, the father stepped outside and said, "Hey, son! You're using it backwards. Turn it around and it will make everything bigger." The little guy answered, "I know that, Dad, but right now I'm looking at the bully who lives down the street. When I look at him this way, it makes him so small that I'm not afraid of him anymore."

Sometimes we simply have to choose to see things differently. We may need to turn our telescopes around because we are magnifying the wrong thing. Problems or challenges become larger when we look at them through the wrong lens. A focus on the wrong thing may convince you that things are never going to work out for you. However, if you'll turn it around, you will see it from a better perspective.

Are you magnifying the wrong thing? Is looking at your problem the wrong way causing you to be fearful and stuck? Is that fear causing you to avoid stepping out and doing what God has called you to do? You can't go around magnifying the negative and expect to live in God's highest and best.

The big kid down the street didn't change, but the boy realized that through the right lens he wasn't as big as he seemed. As a result, the fear that had him stuck melted away. There is a word for the way you see your circumstances or challenges. That word is *perspective*. And here is good news. It is always possible to shift your perspective.

....

It is always possible to shift your perspective.

....

I remember hearing a story about a husband and wife who were headed somewhere in their car when they came to a stoplight. As they sat there, a long black limousine passed through the intersection. They both commented on the car almost simultaneously. The wife said, "Ah, someone's getting married!" The husband said, "Oh no, someone died."

Both people saw the same limousine, but the story they thought the car was telling couldn't have been more different. One saw a story of celebration, while the other saw a story of loss and grief. There is great power in training yourself to look for the good. To assume good. To *expect* good.

Perspective affects everything we do. It colors how we view our circumstances and how we perceive other people. The right perspective can spur you to try harder, have more courage, and give you more grit to go after your dreams. Understanding the power of perspective has reminded countless people to view their lives through the lens of gratitude and opportunity. And I'm sure you've heard the old saying "Attitude determines altitude."

The way we look at life can have a lot to do with how successful we are, how we manage relationships, and what we do with opportunity. It can determine how we walk through difficult seasons. Our perspective is the key to how well we navigate the ups and downs of life. The wrong perspective can cause you to settle for less than God's best. It can have a negative effect on your relationships and make life harder than it should be.

Do you recall the story of the woman with the alabaster jar of precious anointing oil that she poured out on Jesus' feet (Matthew 26)? Some people in the room saw her gesture as a terrible waste of money. Jesus saw the very same thing as a beautiful act of worship. Same event. Two different perspectives. Only Jesus had eyes to see the good that day.

On another day, Jesus and His disciples were faced with a need to feed thousands of people (John 6). The disciples saw a huge hungry crowd and a little boy's sack lunch. But Jesus saw in that same lunch something that could grow into a feast that would feed them all with plenty left over. The disciples started with the wrong perspective, but by the end of the day, their perspective had certainly shifted.

One of my favorite examples of a shift in perspective in the Bible is found in 2 Kings chapter six. The prophet Elisha and his helper were in a dire situation. The two were on a journey in the countryside and woke up one morning to find themselves surrounded by an angry enemy army. Elisha's helper looked around and saw thousands of armed soldiers on horses and in chariots who would love to kill them. The young man was terrified, yet Elisha seemed perfectly calm:

> "Oh no, my lord! What shall we do?" the servant asked.
>
> "Don't be afraid," the prophet answered. "Those who are with us are more than those who are with them." (2 Kings 6:15b–16)

In other words, Elisha said, "Relax. We have them out-numbered." How could he say that? The very next verse tells us:

And Elisha prayed, "Open his eyes, Lord, so that he may see." Then the Lord opened the servant's eyes, and he looked and saw the hills full of horses and chariots of fire all around Elisha. (v. 17)

Elisha was graced with eyes to see something his helper couldn't. Heavenly help was all around them. The same is true for you and me in every situation. The situation that seems so scary isn't scary at all if our eyes are open to the *full* reality. The God who loves to help His people overcome obstacles is always present, even though we often can't see it with our physical eyes. The Father who delights in giving His people victory over giants never leaves us or forsakes us. The One with the power to give breakthroughs is never far away and always ready to respond to faith and trust.

Are you facing a giant? Turn your telescope around. Do you feel outnumbered and surrounded? Ask God for eyes to see the bigger, fuller reality. Are you in the midst of what looks like a negative situation? Choose to have eyes to see the good.

LIFE IS GOOD

A famous author once joked, "The optimist sees the doughnut. The pessimist sees the hole."* There's a lot of truth in that. Our perspective, our mind-sets, the way we choose to look at things, has a huge impact on our enjoyment of life.

When I think about that truth, I think about Bert and John Jacobs, the founders of the successful clothing company built on the saying "Life is good." The boys grew up in a family of eight in a tiny house in Boston. Times were often tough for the family. While the boys were still in grade school, their parents were in a serious car crash. Their father lost the use of his right hand. Frustration over the loss changed something in the boys' father for a time, making him angry and short-tempered. Things were often tense in their household.

But during their growing-up years, their mother had a dinner-table tradition that kept the family positive and

---

* Oscar Wilde.

light. At the Jacobs household, no one stuck a fork into their food until each member of the family related something *good* that happened that day.

Knowing this was coming at the end of the day put all six of the Jacobs children, Bert and John included, on the lookout for good things throughout each day.

The Jacobs brothers learned from their mother that life is not always easy. It's not always perfect. But life is good! And it is that lesson that came to the boys later in life when they needed a fresh idea for their t-shirt company. That is how the incredibly successful "Life is Good" clothing line was born.

We need to be reminded to look on the bright side. You may not have had a parent in your life that instilled a positive attitude in your heart. Maybe you didn't rehearse the good so you could see life with a different lens. The Jacobs brothers would tell you today that life doesn't have to be perfect to be good.

That's why I love this story. I love how their mother taught them to look for the good in every day and in every circumstance, just as my mother did for me. That's a gift I hope to pass to you as you read this chapter. I hope you'll come to understand that life is not perfect but it's good. It's good to be alive. And the truth of Romans 8:28 is always in effect for you as a child of God: "And we know that in all things God works for the *good* of those who love him..."

That means you can always choose to find the good in your circumstances. You can look for the good in your setback. You can find good things in the person who seems to be your biggest critic. It's a choice. And you can train yourself in such a way that it becomes a habit—your natural response to any and every situation.

....

You can always choose to find the good in your circumstances.

....

The opposite of this lifestyle is chronic negativity. Have you ever heard the saying "Look on the bright side"? Or that there is a "silver lining" to every cloud? As clichéd as those old sayings are, they still contain a powerful truth. It is up to us to choose how we are going to view our life. It is something we all must do. It's all about perspective. We all only have this one life, and we don't want to get to the end and think, "If only I had seen it differently."

For years, I have watched my husband, Joel, roll out of bed every morning and say, "It's going to be a great day today!" I must have heard those words thousands of times in the thirty-eight years we have been married. I always thought it was sweet, but I will never forget the morning that what he was doing really sank in for me. On that day I realized Joel was setting the tone for his day. It wasn't just a nice thing to say; he was aligning his thoughts with God's thoughts. He was recognizing he was "graced to go with eyes to see the good."

Scripture says, "This is the day that the Lord has made..." (Psalm 118:24 ESV). Every morning you have a choice. You can rise with your thoughts set on all you have to do that day. You can get up magnifying the big problem you'll be facing at work. Or you can get up with a heart filled with gratitude that you get to have one more day on this Earth and with eyes looking for good things. Eyes that magnify God's goodness and power to carry you through.

Just as the Jacobs brothers' mom and my mother taught us to see the good, you may have had a parent who chronically looked for the bad around every corner and who magnified the problem rather than the solution. Those negative "lenses" often get passed down to the next generation.

I heard a great story about two neighboring farmers. One was always positive and the other chronically negative. When it would rain, the positive farmer would say,

"Lord, thank You for watering our crops." The negative farmer would say, "Yeah, but if it keeps this up, it's gonna rot the roots." When the sun came out, the positive farmer would say, "Lord, thank You for giving our plants valuable sunshine." The negative farmer would say, "Yeah, but if it keeps it up, it's gonna scorch the crops." One day, they went bird hunting together in a boat. The optimistic farmer had just acquired a new bird dog and was so proud of him. Eventually, he shot a duck flying overhead and the bird fell in the water about fifty feet away. He turned to Mr. Negative and said, "Now watch this," and gave the dog a nod. The dog then jumped out of the boat, ran across the top of the water, picked the bird up with its mouth, ran back on top of the water, and dropped it in his owner's lap. Beaming with pride, the dog's owner said, "What d'you think?" The negative farmer shook his head and said, "I should have known it. That dog can't even swim."

It's easy to tell yourself, "When my child gets her life straightened out, then I will have a good day." Or, "When I finally get out of debt, my days will be good ones." Or, "If only my husband would change his ways, it would be easy to find good in my days." All of these and a thousand other excuses only put "seeing the good" off to some future time when things are different. That's not the way God wants us to live. He wants us to see the good in *today* no matter what the present circumstances look like. He wants us to align our thoughts with His thoughts.

So let me ask you: How do you view the difficulties of life? Are you naturally positive or do you find yourself worrying and frustrated with the situations you face? Does the passing limousine cause you to think *funeral* or *wedding*? It matters because research suggests that those who choose to focus on the good adapt better to stressful situations and are able to cope better with life's challenges.

How can we develop this mind-set when we live in a world that is so full of fear, challenges, and hardship? After all, most of us carry around a device with us all day that brings us a constant stream of alarming, scary, or sad news. Paul gives us insight to help us through the tough times and appreciate the good things in life.

Whatever is true, whatever is noble, whatever is right, whatever is pure, whatever is lovely, whatever is admirable—if anything is excellent or praiseworthy—think about such things. (Philippians 4:8)

What we think about sets the atmosphere for our lives. When we constantly dwell on the negative, we can't help but see people and situations through that same dark lens. What we think about and how we think about it is what is going to get on the inside of us. God wants us to train our thoughts to see the good. He wants us to focus on and magnify the good, so we don't give our life over to negativity.

....

> What we think about and how
> we think about it is what is going
> to get on the inside of us.

....

CULTIVATE A "DIFFERENT SPIRIT"

One of the clearest of contrasts of these two choices of mind-set in the Bible involves the Israelites after God miraculously delivered them from slavery in Egypt. Generations of mistreatment had left them feeling victimized and negative. But God wanted to help them change their pattern so they could be blessed.

He promised to bring them into a wonderful land of their own and performed miracle after miracle in the process of rescuing them. Yet they had a hard time shaking off the negativity habit and seeing their circumstances differently. He first brought them out with plenty of wealth and supplies for the journey. He parted the Red Sea for them so they could escape Pharaoh's army, and then they watched as that army was swallowed up so it could never be a threat to them again. You'd think that witnessing this kind of miracle would give you a pretty positive perspective on life.

But in spite of all this, the Israelites continued to instantly go "negative" the moment they hit a new challenge. No matter how many times God supplied food or water or miraculous guidance, they still threw their hands up in despair and complained the moment they came upon a new obstacle. This continued right up to the day they came to the Promised Land.

When they got to the border, God clearly and plainly promised that He would go before them and give the victory over every enemy and obstacle they would encounter (Exodus 33:14). But that apparently wasn't enough assurance, because the Israelites decided to send in twelve spies to explore the land and report back about the new home God had prepared for them. As you may remember, ten of those spies came back saying, basically, "Yes, the land is as wonderful as we'd been told. But there are giants in the land. They're too big for us. We can't defeat them. We're like 'grasshoppers' in their sight." When the rest of the population heard that scary report, they were afraid. Their mind-sets immediately shifted from excitement to despair. From hope to fear. From a victory mind-set to a defeat mind-set.

Please note: I said that was the report of *ten* of those twelve spies. So what about the other two, Joshua and Caleb? They visited the same places the other ten spies visited. They saw the same things the others saw. But they didn't come back talking about obstacles. They came back talking about opportunities. They didn't magnify the problem. They magnified the promise. In Numbers 14:24, God says that Caleb had a "different spirit" than all those Israelites that had the wrong mind-set. This is why, out of that entire generation, only Joshua and Caleb actually entered into the land of promise.

Joshua and Caleb had to align their thoughts with God's. They, like the other spies, had a choice between seeing the problem as too big ("We're like grasshoppers!") and seeing their God as much bigger ("He said He would be with us, so we are well able to take it!" Numbers 13:30). All but two chose the negative perspective. And because of that negative mind-set, what should have been an eleven-day journey from Egypt to the Promised Land actually took forty years.

The Israelites' number one enemy was not the desert, not the need for water and food, not even the seemingly powerful nations and tribes they met along the way. It was their attitude. A wrong perspective was what delayed their entry into all the good things God had prepared and promised.

GO!

So what is your mind-set concerning your own personal "Promised Land"? That land is the life you've dreamed of. It's the life of purpose and meaning and significance and fulfillment your heart longs for and knows you were created for. Like Caleb, you can choose to have "a different spirit," too. You can declare, "Because God is with me, I am well able to *go* and possess the land!"

Go with eyes to see the good. Go with a focus on the opportunities, not the obstacles. Go amplifying what God has said about you, not what others or your own, critical inner voice is saying. Only you can slow and delay your arrival in the good land God has prepared for you.

The happiest people in the world are those who have learned to live this way. They have trained their minds and their hearts to reframe their circumstances and to keep the right perspective. Instead of grumbling and complaining, they stay grateful and count their blessings. Instead of seeing the cloud, they look for the silver lining. Instead of collapsing in disappointment when things don't go their way, they search for and find the "Romans 8:28" *good* in what seems to be a setback.

Empower your life with positive thoughts. Don't short-circuit your abilities with a negative attitude. God has called you higher. So rise up and become a person who knows how to wade into a heap of difficulty and mine gold and treasure out of it.

Jesus said, "In this world you will have trouble. But take heart! I have overcome the world" (John 16:33). With Jesus on your side, you, too, are an overcomer. Life may not be perfect, but it is good. You just have to change the way you see it. Yes, there will be hard seasons, but you have the power of choice about how you view it.

You can choose to see yourself as a victim. You can opt to view life as unfair and stay right where you are. Or you can believe you are graced to GO.

Grace Thoughts

- I remember there is always more than one way to look at my circumstances and at the people around me. I reframe. I find the good.

- When I face things that are trying to limit me or stand in my way, I remind myself that my God is big, that He is *for* me, and that He is working everything for my good.

- When I'm battling fear, I'll "turn my telescope around," knowing that what I magnify matters.

- I know the way I look at life impacts my success in life. I'll not settle for less than God's best.

- I stay mindful that although life is not perfect, it's good. It's good to be alive. And the truth of Romans 8:28 is always in effect for me as a child of God.

- I know that what I think about sets the atmosphere in my life. So I focus on the good and expect good things.

Grace Reflections

1. There is always more than one way to look at my circumstances. How can I shift my perspective of a situation that seems negative right now?

   ....

   ....

2. What I magnify matters. Is there a problem or obstacle in my life that I'm magnifying?

   ....

   ....

3. Elisha was graced with eyes to see something his helper couldn't. Heavenly help was all around them. Have I asked God to open my eyes to see all the help that He wants to make available to me?

   ....

   ....

4. When I think about my "personal promised land," what does it look like?

   ....

   ....

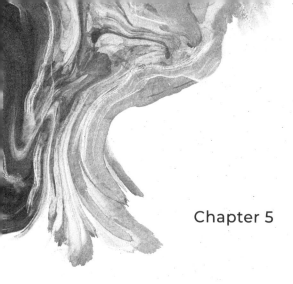

Chapter 5

GO RELEASING
YOUR BLESSING

Let's step into the twelfth chapter of Genesis and put ourselves in the shoes of Abraham and Sarah.

All you ever wanted as a couple was a child. A legacy. Someone to carry on after you're gone. But now you are both well up in years and it seems all hope of having a baby has gone. Then one day the Lord appears to you with amazing news. The best news you've ever received. Not only are you promised a baby, but you also receive a promise that your legacy will be bigger than you could have ever imagined when God says, "I will make you into a great nation" (Genesis 12:2a).

And if that wasn't enough good news for one visit, God goes on to say,

> "…and I will bless you; I will make your name great, and you will be a blessing…and all peoples on earth will be blessed through you." (Genesis 12:2b, 3b)

In the same sentence in which God tells Abraham that He is going to bless him, God also says, "and you will be a blessing." Notice, the two blessings are tied together. They go hand in hand.

It is God's nature to bless you, first of all because He is good and He loves you. But also, so you can extend those blessings to others. The blessing is not supposed to stop with us. As Jesus said in Matthew 10:8, "Freely you have received; freely give." When you're committed to being a blessing, God will not only entrust you with more, but your life will be more fulfilling and rewarding. When you begin to see yourself as a person that God has blessed, you will be free to release the blessing to others. We were never designed to be ingrown, only focused on ourselves. That's the reason some people are not happy. The best way to live is not trying to get blessed, but rather asking, "How can I be a blessing?" When you make other people's day, God will always make your day.

Sometimes we don't think we have anything to give. We're convinced we need someone to bless us. But we all have something. You can give a smile, an encouraging word. You can take your elderly neighbor to dinner or call that friend that's not feeling well. Using your gifts, your resources, or your time to serve others is what pleases the heart of God. And it's the seed for greater blessing in your own life.

God entrusts each of us with opportunities, influence, special gifts to build His kingdom and to bless others. The Scripture says, "Each of you should use whatever gift you have received to serve others, as faithful stewards of God's grace in its various forms" (1 Peter 4:10).

When you release that blessing, it's a seed for God to do greater things in your life. This shouldn't be an occasional thing we do, but a lifestyle where we're always looking for ways to serve and bless others. What a difference it would make in our society if more of us took the time to lend a helping hand or offer words of encouragement.

What a positive influence it would have on the next
generation.

....

> When you release that blessing, it's a seed
> for God to do greater things in your life.

....

It's so easy for us to get caught up in our own lives
and so focused on our own needs that we hardly notice
the people around us. Our duties to our jobs and families often produce such a long list of responsibilities that
we don't look up to see people in our path each day that
we can bless. Busyness and stress can cause us to forget
that God has called us to serve one another. More than
ever, this world needs to see and experience—through our
actions—the love and goodness of God.

LEAVE A LEGACY OF
ENCOURAGEMENT

A women called in to my SirusXM radio show. She
wanted to tell me about a time that she and I had crossed
paths. It was an encounter I didn't think much about

at the time, but she had never forgotten it. This caller said:

> "When your son was at the University of Texas, you came into the department store where I was working in Austin. I helped you, and during our conversation I mentioned how I was going through a hard time because my husband was sick in the hospital. The moment you heard that, you stopped everything you were doing and gave me your full attention."

She went on to remind me that I encouraged her and prayed with her right there in the department store. She said, "It meant so much to me and so lifted my heart that I never forgot it. Now I am more aware of other people's needs because of the way you cared for mine."

That had happened seven years earlier. It was just a small thing that cost me nothing but a few minutes of my time. Yet for this woman, it not only helped in a difficult moment, but changed the way she lived going forward. The same can be true for you. Your kindness and service to others is like a stone thrown in a pond. It sends ripples out. It has life-changing effects. It's a simple but powerful way to leave a legacy of love and encouragement wherever you go.

Let me ask you…Who are you serving? Who are you lifting up? Who are you being good to? Be on the lookout for ways that you can be a blessing. God puts people in our path so we can brighten their day. You don't have to go on a mission trip to another country. There are people you can touch and encourage in your everyday life.

When you serve others, you are serving God. When you do it for them, you're doing it for Him. Jesus said, "If you give a cup of cold water to someone in need, you will surely be rewarded." Every time you serve, God sees it. Every time you help others—when you go out of your way to pick up that friend, come early to volunteer at church, or stay late to train a coworker—God is keeping the records. He will be faithful to refresh and renew you as you refresh and renew others.

NOURISHED AND ENERGIZED

I love the story in John chapter four in which Jesus and His disciples had traveled a great distance to a town in Samaria called Sychar.

Jesus and His friends were tired from the long journey.

It was around noon, and they were all hungry, so the disciples went into the town to buy food. Jesus, now alone, sat down at the place called Jacob's Well. This was where the people of the nearby Samaritan village came to draw water for themselves and their livestock. There, Jesus met a woman who was discouraged and lonely.

As He began to talk to her about her life and what she needed most, His love and compassion toward her changed everything she had ever believed about herself. In the span of a single conversation, her life took on new meaning. She gained such new confidence that she ran to the town to talk about the man who knew about all she had been through and didn't judge her, but rather loved her. His life-giving words changed her. She was renewed and felt whole again.

When the disciples returned with the food and began to urge Him to eat something, Jesus said, "I have food to eat that you know nothing about." They began talking to each other, so confused: "Could someone have brought him something while we were away?"

Jesus' response was so meaningful: "My food comes from doing the will of Him who sent Me, to accomplish His work." Jesus was saying, "I get fed by doing what God asks me to do. My nourishment comes from helping people. My food, My strength, My peace, My joy, My satisfaction—it comes when I serve others."

Maybe you've noticed this. Some days you can work all day just doing your usual, necessary things, and at the end of the day you're tired and worn out. But, in contrast, there are the days you get up early to help that coworker finish a project, you swing by the hospital and pray for that friend, you volunteer for the outreach on your day off, or you serve others in other ways. And you discover that, although you should be so tired, you actually feel reenergized. Refreshed. Why is that? You would think it would be just the opposite.

....

**When you do the will of Your Father,
it doesn't drain you, it replenishes you.**

....

This is what Jesus was talking about. When you do the will of Your Father, it doesn't drain you, it replenishes you. It feeds you, body and soul. When you make somebody else's life better, when you lift people, when you help heal those that are hurting, not only are they being blessed, but you're being blessed. No wonder Jesus declared it is more of a blessing to give than receive (Acts 20:35).

FOUR SIMPLE WORDS

I was walking through the hallway right after service one Sunday morning. The service had just ended, so there were hundreds of people in the corridor. I passed a young lady, looked her in the eyes, smiled, and said, "You are so beautiful." It was just a quick, simple encouragement. And we both went on our way.

Several months later, she saw Joel in the reception Lakewood holds for visitors and newcomers after each service. She told him that the four words I had spoken to her that day had touched and changed her. She had just gotten out of an abusive relationship and had been so beaten down verbally and emotionally that she felt worthless and unattractive. She told Joel, "When Victoria said the words, 'You are so beautiful,' it was like a chain around my mind was broken off. Something came back to life on the inside of me."

When Joel told me that story, I was not only happy for that lady, but it did something on the inside of me. I was encouraged and uplifted. It reminded me that I have the ability to use everything God has given me to help others—including a smile and a few kind words. Yes, it was a small thing, but it made a big difference. You never

know what people are going through, the battles they
fight, the struggles and hardships they've endured. When
you take time to care, it not only lifts them, but the blessing comes back to you. A life of giving is a life filled with
joy and purpose.

You can't give something away without it returning to
you. When you feel that impression, that still small voice
telling you to give, to serve, to encourage, don't put it off.
Release your blessing. Sometimes we think something
nice about a person, but our thoughts don't bless anyone.
A blessing is not a blessing until it's spoken. You have to
release it. God wants to use you to help heal the wounded,
lift the fallen, and breathe hope, life, and fresh vision into
those that are struggling. Make it a priority every day to
say, who can I bless? Who can I encourage? How can I
brighten someone's day? When you live to serve, you're
sowing seeds that will come back to you to lift, to encourage, and to brighten your day.

When I think back on it, it would have been so easy
to miss that opportunity. The hallway was crowded. It was
after the second service that Sunday. I had been up early
and had already had a full day. I was tired and ready to
go home, but I took the time to care. Sometimes we feel

like someone should encourage *us*. Maybe it's been a rough week. It's easy to say,

"I'll do it later."

"I will give them a compliment another time."

"I'll go out of my way when I'm not so busy."

You can't give something away
without it returning to you.

No, don't miss an opportunity to be a blessing. One of the best ways to get refueled and reenergized is to take your mind off yourself and do something good for others. When you give, you're going to receive. God makes sure that it will come back to you. This should be a lifestyle. Not where we have to be talked into it, but where we're looking for ways to be a blessing. At home, we're good to our spouse and children. At work, we take our coworker a cup of coffee. We go out of our way to train the new employee. Driving home, we let that car go in front of us. At the grocery store, we compliment the cashier. At the gym, we encourage that friend to pursue their dream, speaking life and hope into their spirit. This is what brings us joy and fulfillment. Living to give and not living to get. Be a blessing, not focused on being blessed. When you make it your priority to serve others, then the blessings will chase you down. God's goodness and favor will come into your life.

WONDER-WORKING WORDS

Sometimes we're waiting to be a blessing. "Once I get further in my career and achieve my goals, then I'll reach back and help someone else." Or, "Once I get my life straightened out and all my problems solved, then I'll encourage my friend who is going through a tough time." The Scripture says, "Don't miss an opportunity to do good." The people in your path each day are not there by accident. God put them there in His divine plan. He's counting on us to make a difference.

Some are lonely, some don't think they can go on, some are discouraged, ready to give up on their dream. On the outside, they look fine, but on the inside they're hurting. You can be a healer. Your words can breathe new life into their spirit. Your kindness—taking them dinner, inviting them to lunch, stopping by with some flowers—those simple acts can be what keeps them going. It lets them know that God hasn't forgotten about them and that there are good days up ahead. Be aware of who's in your path. It's not random. Your steps are being ordered. Release your blessing. Release your encouragement. Release your kindness. You have been graced with the power to heal the hurting, to lift the fallen, to bring fresh vision and new beginnings that will put people back on the road to victory and purpose.

....

Be aware of who's in your path.
It's not random.
Your steps are being ordered.

....

Proverbs says, "Kind words work wonders." We know God is all-powerful, miraculous. We know *He* can work wonders. But it's significant that He said that *we* can work wonders. How do we do it? One way is through kind words. It's not complicated. You don't have to go to seminary, know all the Scriptures, or have a lot of training. The miracle could be in your words. Your words can bring healing and cause people to feel valued and empowered and help them become who they were created to be. One compliment, one kind word can have an impact for a lifetime. I know that in my life, words have put me on my feet and given me the confidence I needed to accomplish what God had put in front of me. When I began speaking to people from the platform, someone's encouraging words were like strength to my soul. I learned to take those words as if God was speaking to me. God uses people and that became a source of strength that God gave me. Let God speak through you and release the blessing He has for others.

This should start in our homes. I love to tell my husband and children, "I love you." "You look beautiful." "I believe in you." "I so appreciate you." "I'm praying for you." I've discovered these little things can make a big difference. Sure, it's great to serve people when you're out in public. That's important. But make sure you keep that habit going when you get home. I've seen people that treat strangers better than they treat their spouse. They're kind and gracious to someone they've never met, but they're harsh and short with their family. I've heard it said, "Bring your best love home." Serve your own family. Every one of us has an emotional bucket that needs to be filled up. When it is full, we feel happy, satisfied, and encouraged. That's why we need to get in the habit of encouraging one another daily. I want to be known as a bucket filler, not a bucket dipper.

As I look back over the last thirty-eight years of my marriage to Joel, I can see how positive words of affirmation have bonded our hearts together and have caused us to bring out the best in each other. The consistent investment of speaking kind words, being good to each other, and looking for ways to help and serve and make life easier has paid off in countless ways. Now we're enjoying the fruit of that—including living happy and fulfilled, and seeing our children blossom and step into their purpose.

It doesn't happen by accident. Keep kind words in your home. Speak blessings, faith, and victory over your family. Joel tells how I have always encouraged him, using my words to speak faith into him. I make it my business to be his greatest cheerleader. Here's the key: Be generous with your compliments and stingy with your complaints. Look at what they are doing right. Anyone can focus on what's wrong with someone. Use your words to nourish the souls of the people you love. Tell your children what they can become. How they are well able to accomplish what God has called them to. You have to call out the seeds of greatness in them. They have enough people telling them what they can't do, how they don't measure up, and that they're not good enough. Be the voice of healing that tells them what they *can* do. How they're made in the image of God, a masterpiece. Gifted, talented, full of potential. Those words will help set the direction for their lives. All some people need is words of faith and victory to be spoken over them. Your kind words can light the fire on the inside. You can be the one to ignite the passion and calling that God has on their life. Speak faith, speak victory, speak destiny over those that God brings across your path. You can work wonders with your words. As you do this for others, God will make sure people will be there to do the same for you.

....

**Be generous with your compliments
and stingy with your complaints.**

....

FIND YOUR TWINKLE

I once attended the birthday party of a seventy-five-year-old man who happened to be extremely wealthy. It was a warm, happy celebration, and I was very taken by this man's engaging presence as he told me about his life, his biggest accomplishments, and what had meant the most to him. As he spoke, it quickly became clear that it wasn't the status, the professional accolades, or the houses, boats, and cars he'd acquired that meant the most to him. What really animated him was recalling the countless opportunities he'd had to use his position and resources to help others. He told me how he loved to go out and just start handing out hundred-dollar bills. He smiled and shrugged as he said, "It's a small thing, but it gives me joy." He had a twinkle in his eye as he went on to talk about how much he loved working with the foundation he'd launched to help children with disabilities.

It was clear that what he valued most in his life was using his gifts in service to others. This man's life reveals a valuable lesson to us all. No matter our status or financial position, each one of us has the capacity for greatness through service.

True greatness is not defined by external achievements or material success. True greatness and fulfillment are based on the impact we have on others and the value we add to them. That's the legacy each of us can leave behind.

Yes, people in the world often value earthly position most. That's because it can be hard to wrap our heads around the truth that Jesus shared with His disciples. Namely, that servanthood is the pathway to prestige and significance in life. Our culture doesn't view service as the key to success. Rather, it thinks success is being the one who is served. This is why we see people stepping over other people in a frantic scramble for position. It's why we see them ignoring, and even hurting, other people to try to gain more power and authority.

GREATNESS FOUND
IN SERVICE

Jesus gave us the ultimate lesson in leadership and success at the Last Supper. As He sat with His disciples, He overheard them arguing among themselves about who was the greatest and speculating about their position and status in His inner circle. If we use our imaginations a little, we can assume they were comparing their qualifications, or who was with Him most often, or how many times they were present when He performed His miracles. As they competed for elevated position among themselves, Jesus understood they hadn't yet grasped the concept of being a great leader. So He did something profound that demonstrated to them what greatness looked like. He rose from the table and astonished the disciples as He prepared to wash their feet. It's important to understand that, in that day and culture, washing people's feet was the role of the lowest, least-important servant in the house.

By washing His followers' feet, Jesus showed them true greatness through service and humility. His example of washing their feet spoke louder than any words He could have spoken to them. The message was, "Serving one another is not below your position. In fact, it is the key to real greatness and authority." He said:

> "The greatest among you will be your servant. For those who exalt themselves will be humbled, and those who humble themselves will be exalted." (Matthew 23:11–12)

He wanted them to understand that it is a privilege to serve others. And that service is what makes us great. Through His loving-kindness, He set the standard. He didn't just teach it; He lived it.

No matter what position or title you may hold on this Earth, you can still use your influence to serve others. You are called and equipped by the greatest leader who ever lived to be a great servant. Wherever you are right now, you are graced to go to be a blessing and make meaningful contributions to the people around you. It's not titles, applause, status, or earthly position that makes life great. It's the position of your heart.

MARBLE MEMORIAL

Years ago, there was an eight-year-old boy named Barry. He lived out in the country. His family was very poor, struggling to make ends meet. One summer morning, he was at a small grocery store staring at the beautiful display of fresh vegetables. Mr. Miller, the older gentleman who owned the store, came over and asked Barry how he was doing. He said, "Fine, Mr. Miller. I'm just admiring the peas." Mr. Miller asked if he wanted some. He said, "No sir, I don't have any money. Just looking." Mr. Miller said, "What do you have that you could trade me for some of those peas?" He reached in his pocket and said, "All I have are these shiny marbles." They were his prized possession. He never went anywhere without them. Mr. Miller asked to look at the marbles. He said, "Wow, they are so beautiful, but the only thing, Barry, is I like red marbles and all you have are blue and green. You take this sack of peas home and the next time you stop by let me see your red marble."

A local businessman was in the store and watched all this take place. It brought a smile to his face. Barry came by two days later and pulled out a red marble. Mr. Miller said, "I don't know, Barry, I think I changed my mind. I think I like blue marbles better. You take this sack of potatoes home and next time you're in, bring me the blue ones again." This happened again and again. For several years Mr. Miller gave him free vegetables, always asking to see a different color marble than the ones Barry had.

Twenty-three years later, Mr. Miller died. During the viewing, three young men in their early thirties came in, one in a suit and two in army uniforms. As they walked to the casket together, they stopped and hugged Mrs. Miller, whispering something in her ear. As she watched them, one by one, place their hands over her husband's hand, tears welled up in her eyes. Later that evening, the businessman that had been in the store all those years before came in and shared with Mrs. Miller how he had seen her husband be so kind to the little boy, giving him vegetables and not taking his marbles. She smiled and told how her husband had repeatedly done that same thing for two other young men as well—always saying it was just not the right color marble.

She then said, "But now my husband, Jim, doesn't have a choice about the color or the size." She walked with the man to the casket and gently lifted up the lifeless hand of her husband. Under it were three shiny red marbles left by the three young men.

Kind deeds are never forgotten. They may seem small to us, but they'll be remembered for a lifetime. Take time to be good to people. Look for ways that you can release your blessing.

BE A SPONGE

To be a truly great giver, you need to know how to be a great receiver. Think about a sponge. It has the capacity to soak things up. And then, when squeezed, it has the ability to give what it has absorbed.

I want to challenge you to be a sponge when it comes to God's goodness and blessings. Expect blessing. Expect His favor. And when it comes, willingly soak it up like a sponge. Receive His blessing, recognizing every good thing comes from our Father in Heaven. Then, at every opportunity, be willing to share that blessing with others. Let what you've soaked up come out. Be an extravagant giver. When you live a life of generosity, you're living your best life.

There is never a time that you are empty-handed. You always have something to give. In the book of Acts, Peter and John were walking to the temple to worship God. It was a time of day when everyone came to worship at the temple. I can just imagine the crowd and everybody trying to get into the temple so they could all get a good seat.

They came across a beggar who had never walked. The poor man cried out to Peter and John for a little money. Maybe you're familiar with Peter's reply to the man.

> Then Peter said, "Silver or gold I do not have, but what I do have I give you. In the name of Jesus Christ of Nazareth, walk." (Acts 3:6)

The two disciples didn't have a penny between them. But they did have something to give. We always have something to give. I have a prayer. I have a hand. I have a word. I have something I can do for you. I always have something I can give to you—even if it's just time. The truth is, time is the scarcest, most valuable resource of all.

You are never empty-handed. When you serve others, you are serving God. What you do for them you are doing for Him. Jesus said, "If you give a cup of water to someone in need, you will surely be rewarded."

Nothing you do for others goes unnoticed by God. Don't miss an opportunity to be good to others. Friend, you are graced to go. As you release your blessing, God is going to release His goodness in your life in ways that you've never imagined.

....

As you release your blessing, God is going
to release His goodness in your life
in ways that you've never imagined.

....

Grace Thoughts

- I am blessed to be a blessing. And because I am a blessed person, I will bless others.

- I always have something I can give to others. I have a smile, a kind and encouraging word. I am never empty-handed, so I will release a blessing to those around me.

- I serve others gladly and with joy, knowing that it is the key to a joyful life full of purpose.

- Like a sponge, I soak up good things as God brings them to me. And I stay ready to share them with others.

- When I serve others, I am serving God. What I do for them I am doing for Jesus.

- Nothing I do for others goes unnoticed by God. He rewards and refreshes me as I do good to others.

Grace Reflections

1. Kind words work wonders. So who can I be a wonder-worker for today?

   ....

   ....

2. What am I waiting for? Have I been thinking that I will bless and encourage others only when I attain a higher position, more influence, or more resources?

   ....

   ....

3. Who am I serving? Who am I lifting up? Who am I being good to? Am I on the lookout for ways that I can be a blessing to people God puts in my path so I can brighten their day?

   ....

   ....

4. Do I feel overlooked or unseen? Am I mindful that no good thing I do goes unnoticed by God?

   ....

   ....

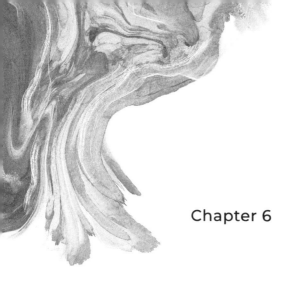

GO WITH NO REGRETS

Joel's dad was married at a young age and, unfortunately, the marriage didn't work out. He was a pastor of a denominational church at that time and knew a divorce meant they would ask him to resign. He felt guilty and ashamed. He was sure his life in ministry was over, so he stepped down. He heard an accusing voice in his head saying, "You will never pastor again. You will never have the big family you always wanted." He felt unworthy and completely disqualified.

For two years he sat on the sidelines, not pursuing the call of God on his life to minister. Instead, he sold insurance and beat himself up because he felt like a failure in his marriage. The accusing voice of the enemy told him that if he couldn't help his own marriage, how could he help anyone else? The Scripture calls the enemy an "accuser." He wants to remind you of every mistake you have ever made. He would have loved it if Joel's dad, John Osteen, would have buried his calling and stayed in a place of condemnation.

One night when he was praying, he rose up in his own spirit and asked, "If God sent His son to forgive me of my sins, what good is it if I can't accept His forgiveness for my mistakes and receive the love that He came to give me?" That was a turning point in his life. He knew if he was going to start over, he had to take the next step and forgive himself.

So he did. He asked God for forgiveness and then forgave himself.

He began doing ministry again and ended up marrying Joel's mother, Dodie. They went on to have four great children and one exceptional one. (That's the way Joel sees it, anyway. Of course, I agree. He is exceptional!)

Joel's father didn't let the negative emotion of regret win. And because he didn't, he ended up traveling the world ministering to pastors and was able to build a church that is still going strong some sixty years later. If he hadn't received the grace to let go of his mistake, I wouldn't have experienced traveling with him and ministering to pastors and leaders in many different countries.

Living with the feeling that things could have or should have been different not only impacts *your* life negatively but can rob others of blessings and benefits, too.

IF GOD HAS FORGIVEN YOU

Is regret holding you captive? Are there things in your past that you wish would have turned out differently? Choices you wish you hadn't made? Forks in the road of life you wish you hadn't taken? Yes, a lot of regret centers around things we did but wish we hadn't. But that's not the only source.

We can also carry regret over what we did *not* do but wish we had, including opportunities we passed up and open doors we didn't step through. The great actor John Barrymore once said, "A person is not truly old until regrets take the place of dreams." The fact is, God doesn't want you growing "old" that way—full of regret and sad-ness. His desire is for you to be dreaming, and achieving, and living with passion right up until the day you go to Heaven.

The enemy, on the other hand, would love for you to go through life pitted against yourself. Nothing would make him happier than to keep you trapped in a prison of "woulda, coulda, shoulda." Paralyzed by guilt and con-demnation. Sitting on the sidelines of life watching others move forward and achieve success. Always looking back. Never stepping forward in faith. Here is the thing: When you ask God to forgive you, He forgives you. But that isn't the end of the process. You must then move to the next phase and forgive yourself. That's one of the most impor-tant first steps to letting go of regret.

The Apostle Paul understood this so well. He said, "…one thing I do, forgetting what lies behind and strain-ing forward to what lies ahead. I press on toward the goal of the high calling of God in Christ Jesus."

If you know Paul's backstory, you will understand why that is such a significant thing for him to say. Before God changed his name from Saul to Paul, Saul of Tar-sus had been persecuting Christians. He actually led the effort to persecute the new Jesus movement in its early years, dragging Christians out of their homes so they could be beaten, jailed, and even killed. When Stephen, the first Christian to die for the faith, was stoned to death, Saul/Paul was there looking on with approval. After Jesus appeared to him, changed his heart, and rewrote his story, Paul looked back on that time in his life with deep feelings of guilt, shame, and regret.

Paul had this painful personal experience in mind when he wrote those words in Philippians: "…forgetting what lies behind." He knew he had to remind himself that God loved him and had called him, and to not allow his past mistakes to hold him back and occupy his thoughts. But it's not enough to just forget the mistakes of the past. He also said "…straining forward to what lies ahead…" The words Paul used indicate that it was a challenge. "Straining" suggests exercise. His faith muscles were being developed. Then he said, "I *press* on toward the goal of the high calling of God in Christ Jesus."

Paul had to press. In other words, it wasn't an easy thing. He had to be willing to accept God's forgiveness and then forgive himself. Only then could he receive grace to move forward without regrets. Could it be that this was a constant test of his faith? Was it a struggle to go boldly into what God had called him to do instead of looking back in regret and shame? It seems that Paul knew regret was the enemy of moving into the good things God had called him to do and be.

Here's my question for you...

If Paul needed grace to go with no regrets, isn't it likely that you and I do, too?

Sure, for most of us, unlike Paul, our past mistakes don't involve having killed and imprisoned innocent Christians or having acted mercilessly in the name of God. But we can still feel the sting of regret. We still blame ourselves for a bad outcome. Maybe there is a sense of sorrow for what might have been, or a wish we could go back and undo a previous choice. Maybe it is regret from the way we treated a loved one. Regret about the decision not to go to college. Or missing an opportunity that we let pass by.

There are so many possible reasons to feel regret. And if those negative feelings are not handled correctly, they tend to steal our strength and make us feel helpless in those areas. Paul sensed that. He knew he could never successfully complete his "race" weighted down with regret. So he released his burden of regret to Jesus and received, by faith, the gift of forgiveness. This produced the wholeness and healing he needed to move forward with the assignments God had given him. This is the same Paul who,

in 2 Corinthians 7:10, tells us that Godly sorrow leaves
no regret. He repented, received forgiveness, put the past
behind him, and, refusing to look back, pressed on toward
his new life in Jesus Christ.

LOOK FORWARD, NOT BACK

We all make mistakes. We all have things in the past we
wish would have been different. But we weren't created to
live in that space. We can't truly thrive in that space. Sure,
the enemy would love for you to spend your days feeling
condemned. He'll happily remind you of all the times you
haven't measured up. He'll be delighted if he can keep you
looking back over your shoulder in regret and shame.

He doesn't really care whether it's something big or
just small things. Maybe you didn't spend enough time
with your children last week. Maybe you skipped a work-
out. Or got mad at your neighbor. You were late to school.
There is never a shortage of reasons to feel bad about who
we are and what we have (or haven't) done. If you fall into
this condemnation and shame trap, you'll go through life
constantly feeling wrong on the inside. It steals your confidence and limits your ability to step out past where you
are right now. In other words, it keeps you "stuck."

God doesn't want us held hostage in our thoughts to what could have been. He makes all things new! And He has graced us to move forward without the sting of shame or the heavy weight of regret. When you live in regret, you've already made up your mind about what is possible. You've decided in advance what will happen next based on a past experience you have already defined in your mind as failure. I frequently heard Joel's dad say, "God doesn't make any failures, only learners." In more recent times some have said, "There's no failure. Only feedback." The great inventor Thomas Edison is reported to have said, "I never view mistakes as failures. They are simply opportunities to find out what *doesn't* work." Those are statements we all need to adopt if we are going to go into the new and better things God has in store for us.

....

He has graced us to move forward
without the sting of shame or the
heavy weight of regret.

....

I've found most people are far quicker to accept condemnation than they are to accept mercy. Because we know our own hearts and histories so well, we swallow lies from the accuser but are slow to believe what God says about us. And God says you're forgiven. That you're redeemed. That you've been declared worthy.

Yes, we all make mistakes. We'll blow it from time to time. When you do, go to God, ask for forgiveness, take Him at His Word, and then move on. You can't be a servant to regret—letting it paralyze you or to shrink back out of fear of making another mistake. Instead, choose to live in the freedom and grace that is abundantly, extravagantly yours in God.

GOD IS ALWAYS AT THE WINDOW

One summer, a nine-year-old boy named Sam and his older sister visited their grandparents on their farm. He brought along a slingshot he'd recently received for his birthday. Throughout those long, lazy days of summer, Sam would walk through the woods launching pebbles at different targets. He wasn't very accurate, but he kept practicing.

One evening, he heard the dinner bell ringing and headed for the house. As he neared the farmhouse, he spotted his grandmother's pet duck way over by the pond—roughly fifty yards away. Sam didn't think he had a chance in the world of hitting it. But just for fun, he pulled the slingshot back as far as he could and let a pebble fly. Much to his surprise, it hit the duck square in the head, knocking it over dead. In a panic, Sam ran over as quick as he could, grabbed the duck, and buried it under some leaves behind the woodpile.

He felt terrible about it, but he wasn't about to say anything to his grandparents. When he got close to the house, he realized, to his dismay, that his twelve-year-old sister Julie had witnessed the whole thing. He also knew that Julie enjoyed getting him in trouble and also wasn't above engaging in blackmail. In fact, that night after dinner, the grandmother said, "Julie, let's you and me wash the dishes together tonight." With a gleam in her eye, Julie said, "Grandmother, I would love to, but Sam said he wants to help you tonight." Then she whispered in Sam's ear, "Remember the duck," while giving him a look of warning.

Sam dutifully went over and washed the dishes in her place. The next morning, the grandfather was going fishing and invited both children to come. The grandmother said, "I really need Julie to stay here and help me do some chores." Again, Julie smiled and said, "Grandmother, Sam said he really wants to stay with you today." Again, she shot

Sam a look that said, "Remember the duck." So Julie went fishing while Sam stayed behind and worked. After a couple of days of doing both his and his sister's chores, Sam had finally had enough of the blackmail. He went to his grandmother and said, "Grandmother, I have to tell you something. I accidentally killed your pet duck with my slingshot, and I'm very sorry."

The grandmother gave him a big hug and said, "Oh, Sam, I know. I was standing at the window and watched the whole thing happen. I know you didn't mean to. I already forgave you. I was just waiting to see how long you were going to let Julie make a servant of you."

There is a powerful lesson there for you and me. God is always standing at the window. He's seen every mistake, every failure, every weakness. And He is always ready and eager to forgive. In fact, Jesus bore our sins and the guilt of them on the cross two thousand years ago. That means that, whatever you've done, He's not holding it against you. He's just waiting to see how long you're going to let the accuser make a servant of you.

How long are you going to live with that guilt, believing that you've blown your chance at a good future? How long are you going to ask forgiveness over and over for the same mistakes? I encourage you to make this declaration.

"No more. This is a new day!" We're going to rise up like Sam did and say, "Enough is enough." Let's rise up like my father-in-law, John Osteen, did all those years ago and say, "Yes, I've made some mistakes, but I'm not going to go through life condemned, trying to pay a debt that's already been paid, thinking that I've missed my destiny. I'm going to arise."

Receive and believe this wonderful news. You can still become all you were created to be. No mistake you've made is too much for the mercy and grace of God. But you *must* choose to believe that, and then get back in the game.

....

No mistake you've made is too much for the mercy and grace of God.

....

SILENCE THE ACCUSER

No doubt you can look back and see times where you gave in to temptation. We all can. You let your guard down and compromised. You were stressed out and didn't handle the situation the way you wish you had. It's easy to end up defined by a bad time in life. Or by a divorce. Or a business that didn't make it. Or a choice that set you back.

Whatever your mistakes and regrets from the past, you can be sure the enemy is happy to remind you of them. He's called "the accuser" for a reason. He would love to convince you to let that one mistake, that one season, that wrong turn, cause you to live constantly down on yourself. And doing that will rob you of your passion for your dreams. But here's the truth: That mistake didn't stop God's plan. You may have failed, but you are not a failure. That was a moment in your life. That was one season. Just one part of one chapter in a story God is still writing. That thing you regret doesn't determine your future. Don't let that mistake define who you are. If you go around wearing negative labels—Divorced, Addicted, Failed, Compromiser—it will keep you from the fullness of what God has in store. Instead, receive grace to go forward with no regrets.

This is what happened to Moses. When he was a young man, God gave him the dream that he would deliver the Israelites out of slavery. He knew he was supposed to do it but he got in a hurry and did it out of God's timing. He saw a Hebrew slave being mistreated by an Egyptian supervisor. He didn't think anyone was watching and he killed the supervisor. Moses wasn't trying to make a mistake. He wasn't being defiant; he just made a bad choice in the emotional heat of the moment. But he had to flee for his life. He spent forty years on the backside of the desert in hiding.

It looked like that one mistake had stopped his destiny. It seemed that that one bad choice had disqualified him. Can you imagine his thoughts and "self-talk" out in the desert? "Moses, you're a failure. What were you thinking? Why are you so impatient? You blew it!" He was wearing all these negative labels. He thought that mistake would define him.

The good news is, God doesn't judge us by one mistake, or by two mistakes, or for some of us by ten thousand mistakes. God's calling on your life is irrevocable. He doesn't change His mind. Moses had given up. Written himself off. He had accepted that he would never accomplish his dream, but he eventually discovered that God doesn't give up. Like Moses, you may have counted yourself out. But the truth is, God has already counted you *in*. He chose you before you could choose Him. That past mistake is not who you are; it's just something you did. It didn't cancel your destiny. That one bad season doesn't determine the rest of your life.

Moses discovered that, forty years after committing murder, when he was eighty years old, God still had a plan for his life. His destiny wasn't in the desert but it was to deliver the people out of the hands of the Pharaoh. I can imagine Moses said, "God, are You sure? You mean after I've failed? After I blew it? After I was impatient, You're still going to use me?"

God's calling on your life is irrevocable. He doesn't change His mind.

Here's the good news. God doesn't *define* us by our mistakes. He *refines* us by our mistakes. He will take those failures and wrong turns and use them to do a work in us. He doesn't waste anything. Believe you are graced to go. Get your fire back. Get your passion back. Quit believing the lie that it's too late. Or that you've made too many poor choices. Stop telling God everything you've done wrong. If you want to get God's attention, go to Him with boldness. Dare to ask Him for favor—despite the mistakes you've made. Dare to ask Him to open new doors and to take you where you couldn't go on your own. Is that audacious? Yes, it is. Which reminds me of the story of one of the most significant people in the Old Testament, Jacob.

Scripture tells us he had lived his whole life being dishonest and cheating people. In fact, he scammed his own brother out of his birthright and tricked his own father into giving him his brother's rightful inheritance. But he finally got tired of living that way. One night, he went down to the brook by himself to get alone with God to make things right. An angel appeared in the form of a man. Jacob started wrestling with him. This went on all night. Jacob finally realized it was an angel. He said to him, "I'm not going to let you leave until you bless me." When the angel saw how determined Jacob was, how he wasn't going to give in, he touched Jacob and gave him the blessing. That night, God changed his name from Jacob to Israel. He left there a different person. Jacob understood the mercy of God.

After all those years of cheating people and making bad choices, he should have been living under a heavy burden of guilt and feeling totally unworthy. But somehow, he had the boldness to not only ask for forgiveness but to say, "God, I'm asking You to bless me, despite what I've done wrong." He didn't deserve forgiveness, much less to be blessed. But God saw his sincere heart of repentance.

He likes it when we come to Him in faith, with boldness, believing that He is merciful and that He doesn't hold our past mistakes against us.

If God would bless Jacob after living that kind of life, why are you believing the lies that God won't bless you? That you don't deserve it? That you're not worthy? That you're disqualified because of the choices you made?

Do yourself a favor: Quit telling God all about your mess-ups and failings and instead go to Him like Jacob did. Say, "Father, I thank You that You are full of mercy. So I'm asking You to bless me, not because of how good I am, but because of how good You are."

That's what gets God's attention. That's what He listens to.

How much time are you wasting being down on yourself? How much of your life are you spending beating yourself up over past mistakes and telling God what you *don't* deserve? That's a lot of emotional energy that's not doing you or anyone else any good.

Yes, God hears you. Sure, He knows you're sincere. But He's not moved by our guilt. He's moved by our faith. It takes faith to believe you're forgiven. It takes faith to not only believe for your dreams, but to believe that you're worthy of achieving them. Don't let the accuser deceive you into going through life with no dreams and no passion because you think you've blown it too many times. Your record has been cleared. Those files have been deleted. Now, do like Jacob and come boldly to the throne.

GET GOING

I think it's so significant that after Jacob's "wrestling" encounter, God changed Jacob's name (which had a negative meaning) to Israel, which means "Let God prevail." There's a lesson in that for you and me.

Don't let regrets from the past prevail. Let God prevail. He is the one who sits on the throne. He is the one who gives us His grace and mercy. He is the one who gave us His best so we could rise and do our best. Let God prevail and your enemies be scattered. When, instead of letting regret prevail, we come boldly to God and surrender ourselves to Him, putting Him on the throne of our lives, wonderful things happen. The enemy called regret can't thrive when you bring all to God.

Sure, we all make mistakes. We will say something we later wish we hadn't. We'll act unkindly. And when that happens, the accuser will be quick to say, "There you go again." But instead of falling back into that place of condemnation, just be a quick learner. Repent, ask for forgiveness, learn from the mistake, and move on. Don't stay down and discouraged—it will only lead to more regret.

For example, one Christmas we went out of town to celebrate with family and friends. I knew I was going to be off my regular eating schedule and that there were going to be plenty of holiday goodies that would be tempting. So I prepared myself to be disciplined. I promised myself that I wasn't going to eat all that junk and gain weight. I was going to stick to my plan, exercising in the morning and passing on all the cookies and candy that I would be so tempted to eat.

I did have a great holiday and thoroughly enjoyed my friends and family. But when I got home, to my shock and disappointment, I had gained about five pounds. This was on top of the five pounds I had already wanted to drop before we left. As the disappointment and regret set in, I made the mistake of getting down on myself. Which, in turn, drained all my motivation and energy to go to the gym or even to take brisk walks in the neighborhood. But that's not all it stole. I lost sight of all the good memories from the holiday. That's the cycle of regret.

I had to release it. I began to encourage myself that I was not a failure, and that I was going to learn from this and do better, and I found a new strength. My motivation came back, and I began to improve my habits. It is amazing what will happen if you let go of the past choices and decide that you are still graced to go forward. That you still have a bright future. That's allowing God to prevail. And He sees you as an overcomer, not as a person who is overcome by bad choices, mistakes, and the things that didn't work out. He calls you more than a conqueror because of what He did for you.

No one is perfect, so if you find yourself discouraged because of choices you've made—you didn't finish the project, you said something you shouldn't have—don't stay stuck in regret. Ask for forgiveness, forgive yourself, and move forward. Let yourself off the hook.

....

**God has graced you to go with
no regrets, so you can become
all you were meant to be.**

....

Take John Barrymore's advice. Don't let regrets replace your dreams. God has graced you to go with no regrets, so you can become all you were meant to be.

Grace Thoughts

+ I don't let regrets take the place of my dreams. God's desire is for me to be dreaming, and achieving, and living with passion right up until the day I go to Heaven.

+ When I mess up, instead of falling back into that familiar place of condemnation, I'm a quick learner instead. I repent, learn from the mistake, and move on.

+ I know that if Paul needed grace to go with no regrets, I surely do, too. I receive that grace.

+ I know God makes all things new! And He has graced me to move forward without the sting of shame or the heavy weight of regret.

+ I will not stay stuck in regret. I'll ask for forgiveness, forgive myself, and move forward.

+ God's calling on my life is irrevocable. He doesn't change His mind. So I'll never count myself out. God has already counted me *in*.

Grace Reflections

1. "Because we know our own hearts and histories so well, we swallow lies from the accuser but are slow to believe what God says about us." Am I quicker to accept condemnation or to accept mercy?

   ....

2. God has made all things new for me. So why would I allow myself to be held hostage in my thoughts about what could have been or should have been?

   ....

3. Will I wrestle with an angel? In other words, am I willing to be determined and persevere while moving into who God made me to be and the good things He has prepared for me?

   ....

4. When I make a mistake, do I listen to the voice of condemnation? Or am I quick to repent, ask for forgiveness, learn from the mistake, and move on?

   ....

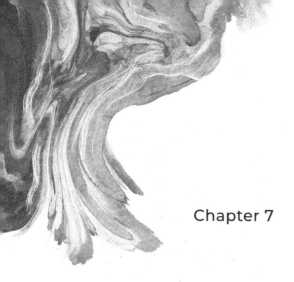

Chapter 7

GO TRUSTING GOD

Years ago, Joel offered a man named Craig Johnson a position at our church. Saying yes would mean relocating his wife and children from California to Houston. It was a big decision, but Craig and his wife, Samantha, knew that God was leading them to Lakewood. They were excited for their family to start the next chapter of their lives.

The Johnsons had three beautiful kids. The older two were Cory and Courtney. It was fun to have them in Houston. I remember how they would come over to our house after church to play with our kids. Their third child, Connor, was a surprise blessing to their family born about a year or so before they moved to Houston.

Throughout the first two years of his life, Connor was an average, well-adjusted, happy child—very much like his older siblings had been at that age. He was engaging and loved to laugh. Then, suddenly, everything changed.

Connor became withdrawn. He stopped showing emotion. Over a period of just a few weeks, the cheery, active little guy they'd known for two years was replaced by someone they didn't know.

Craig and Samantha hoped it was just a strange phase their two-year-old was going through. But when it didn't pass, they went looking for medical answers. Soon, the diagnosis they'd dreaded was delivered: autism.

With a single word, it felt as if all of their aspirations and hopes for Connor's life vanished before their eyes. Craig and Samantha cried out to God repeatedly for answers. During one such time of wrestling with God, Craig was in his car, tears rolling down his face, and asking God, "Why is my son struggling so much?" The answer that came back in his spirit was, *Craig, your child is not a burden. Your child is a gift.*

Then God spoke something else to Craig that he would never have guessed was coming. He clearly heard the Lord say, *I am going to use your son to reach millions of people.* That just didn't make any sense to Craig at all. Confused, he cried out, "Lord, how is my son going to reach millions of people? He can't even ask for a drink of water."

God answered Craig's question with a question of His own. *Do you trust Me?*

Those four words rocked Craig to his core. The issue of trust was at the heart of the two other questions: Would Craig choose to see Connor as a gift? And how would God bring about the "impossible" promise to use Connor to reach and touch millions?

Gathering up all of his faith and trust in God, Craig chose to say yes. To say "Yes, God, I will trust You."

We see many people in the Bible who had to do the same thing. Take Job, for example.

After experiencing incredible devastation, Job called out to God in confusion and pain. He was looking for answers. As you read the book that carries his name, you see him at times angry with God. He shares his heart honestly, but one thing we don't see Job doing is walking away from God. He never doubts that God is there. And he never stops talking to Him.

There is a lesson in there for you and me. When life suddenly feels desolate and unfair, our answer is to run to God, not from Him. We must seek Him and His provision even when we don't understand.

....

**When life suddenly feels desolate
and unfair, our answer is to
run to God, not from Him.**

....

Talk to God. It's okay to be honest. You can tell Him you're angry. You can tell Him you're confused. You can tell Him life doesn't seem fair. Tell Him exactly how you feel, but above all, talk to Him, and keep talking to Him.

That is what Job did and that is what Craig did. I can promise you, if you talk to God, and continue to seek answers from Him, He will talk to you. It's important to turn to Him even in our darkest moments. His presence is where you will find strength and purpose in the midst of the difficulty. He will provide you with the peace and hope to keep going.

EMBRACING THE POSSIBILITIES

With a word from God, Craig and Samantha came to a place where they, together, were willing to follow God's grace and the promise that was in their hearts.

As they trusted God and looked to Him for help, they were inspired and came up with an idea. They knew their older kids loved coming to church and experiencing worship and the teaching that was formatted just for them. They also knew Connor enjoyed children's church but the sensory overload from the singing and noise of the regular formatted service was not something that served his learning style.

Through their journey, they also met other parents of children diagnosed with autism. They discovered that these children, like Connor, struggled. That prompted a question: Why can't there be a version of church specifically designed to minister to autistic children and young people?

Craig and Samantha went to work and crafted a mission statement: "To develop spaces for autistic children and young people that would help them to develop spiritually, emotionally, physically, and creatively."

The Johnsons brought their idea to Joel and me. We put together a team to explore their vision, and out of those conversations the Champions Club was born. We built specially designed rooms to accommodate these children and trained volunteers using a curriculum Craig and Samantha developed. Almost immediately, the Champions Club was at capacity, so we added rooms and volunteers. It enabled parents to attend regular service while their children were learning about God at their own pace.

Soon, other families asked for assistance in ministering to their children with different special needs. So Craig went to work again. Now, the Champions Club serves children, teens, and adults with special needs as well as the medically fragile.

The need was great, but until the Johnsons went through their challenges with Connor, no one realized it. Today, the Champions Club at Lakewood is a beautiful, life-giving success. It has not only brought families to Lakewood Church who might not ever have walked through the doors, but many moved from somewhere else to Houston just to be a part of it.

"That is amazing," you may be thinking, "but wasn't Connor supposed to inspire a vision that would affect the world?"

The answer is, "Yes!" Within a year of opening, other churches around the United States had heard about

Lakewood's Champions Club. Pastors and ministers from all over visited Houston to see it for themselves. They left inspired, and one after another asked Craig and Samantha to help them to establish clubs at their churches. A global ministry was born.

By believing that they were graced to go with exactly what they had—no more, no less—Craig and Samantha have established more than 107 Champions Clubs across the United States and on six continents. They have only begun. God's promise to Craig on a dark and desperate day that Connor's life would bless millions of people is being fulfilled before their eyes.

And what about Connor's story? You'll be blessed to know that the same developmental methods and ministry that God is using to help countless kids and adults through the Champions Club has brought Connor further than his family, or anyone, could have imagined. Today, as a young man in his twenties, Connor has learned to communicate well with others. He has a job and friends, is continuing to grow and thrive, and experiences a full and joyful life, including a love of Jesus and of being at church.

Craig and Samantha chose to embrace God's promise instead of the pain. To embrace new purpose instead of staying stuck in what could have been.

God's grace and mercy can truly work wonders in our lives. Shifting our hearts and minds from hopelessness to the possibilities of what God can do in the hardest places. Craig and Samantha's story is a reminder that God is there with us, guiding us through even the most difficult times. Trusting His plan and allowing His grace to work in our lives can open new doors for God to write a wonderful story of hope and healing.

GIVE GOD SOMETHING TO WORK WITH

Craig and Samantha offered God their faith and obedience. They trusted God to work all things together for good. He saw their efforts and sacrifice and He made something beautiful out of it. We may not always understand why certain things are happening, but we can trust that God has a purpose and a plan for everything, and He is constantly working in our life.

Trusting God when you don't understand why can be a difficult task. It requires a deep level of faith and surrender to God's will when circumstances are overwhelming.

It reminds me of a widow whose story we find in 1 Kings chapter seventeen. During a time of terrible drought and famine in Israel, the prophet Elijah encountered this woman gathering sticks for a fire.

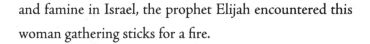

**We can trust that God has a purpose
and a plan for everything, and He is
constantly working in our life.**

When the prophet asked her for a cup of water and some bread, the woman said, "I only have a handful of flour and a little oil left to make one final meal for me and my son." She expected to die of starvation because the famine was so severe.

God knew and cared about this woman's desperate situation. It was no accident the prophet showed up at her place on that day and at that specific time. Elijah then made a request of the woman that made no natural sense. In fact, it seems crazy.

He asked her to go back and use the last of her ingredients to make *him* a meal. After that, according to the prophet's instructions, she was to go back home and prepare a meal for herself and her son. Of course, that second part was impossible if she obeyed the first part. But Elijah added the amazing promise of a miracle to that last part.

The prophet said that if she trusted God and God's messenger, she would never run out of oil or flour until the drought and famine were over. Despite her dire circumstances, the widow demonstrated incredible faith and generosity. She did what the prophet asked and gave him what she had. Trusting in God's plan, she obeyed and in return she experienced miraculous provision in an extreme time. God multiplied her flour and oil so she and her son had more than enough to eat throughout the entire famine.

By offering what we have to God, whether it be our circumstances, finances, or relationships, we demonstrate our reliance on Him as our provider, sustainer, and guide for our life. When we surrender control and are willing to give Him control, He will work in ways beyond what we could ever do. He is able to take what we offer in faith and obedience and use it for His divine purpose. Notice that God helped this woman make the same shifts in focus the Johnsons made. She stepped out with what she had. And she used what she had to meet someone else's need. When she did that, God made sure her needs were met in an amazing way. How about you?

Your setback, disappointment, or situation might not be as extreme as what the Johnsons, or Job, or that widow experienced. But we've all had times when things seemed to be going great and then, with no warning, some bad news pulled the rug out from under us. An unexpected divorce, a child gone off course, or maybe the loss of a job.

If you've experienced this, you know how, in a moment, everything can change. No, it doesn't seem fair. In the midst of confusion, uncertainty, and deep disappointment, you can suddenly feel as if you've lost everything.

I encourage you, like the Johnsons, like Job, to turn to God. Give Him what you have in your hands. It may not seem like much, but you can trust Him with it.

In God's sovereignty and provision, He is able to take what you don't understand and use it for His divine purpose and your good.

HOPE TURNS THE LIGHT ON

In the darkness of a hard place, we can lose sight of what we have. But hope turns on the light so you can see what remains. You have a God with the pen in His hand. That alone is more than enough to keep the spark of hope alive. I've heard it said, "Once you choose hope, anything's possible."

You just have to begin to look for God's hand of favor and trust that this isn't the end and the setback isn't going to define your life. What could have defined the Johnsons' lives was redefined by the hand of God. Job was restored to double. The widow had more than enough to set her and her son on the path to life.

....

Hope turns on the light so
you can see what remains.

....

You do, too. Look around and light up your search with hope. There is always something God can work with. He is always waiting in that something to do bigger and better than what you thought possible. That's the amazing truth discovered by a group of grieving women on a remarkable Sunday morning nearly two thousand years ago.

UNFINISHED BUSINESS

I'm not sure there has ever been a group of women who felt more loss and more darkness than the ones who had followed Jesus for three years—sitting at His feet, watching

Him perform wonders—and then watching as He was crucified that Friday.

As they watched Him die, it must have looked like everything they'd believed in and everything they'd hoped for was over. Those same women prepared Jesus' body for burial on that late Friday afternoon. And because the sun was about to set, religious laws demanded that they had to hurry their work.

So these women, including Mary Magdalene and other close followers and relatives, had to sit behind bolted doors for a night, a day, and then another night. That's a lot of time to stew and soak in disappointment. A lot of time to think about how hopeful and expectant they had been just a few days earlier. Time to get stuck in grief and regret and fear. But that's not what these women did.

They had an unfinished job to do. And they had what they assumed was one last opportunity to honor and minister to the Jesus they loved.

So, with what they had left, they chose to go trusting God. They headed for the tomb where they'd watched a handful of burly men roll a massive circular stone across the entrance. How did they think they were going to move that stone? They must have just decided they'd figure it out when they got there.

Hope is like that. It has an amazing way of pulling you toward things that seem impossible to others. All the other followers of Jesus were hiding and in despair, but these women went to the tomb anyway. There was no reason to think that what they were about to do was going to solve the source of their heartache, but they went to the tomb anyway. There was no way to move that stone, but they went to the tomb anyway.

When they arrived, they found the stone already rolled away. And inside, instead of the hastily wrapped body of their beloved friend and teacher, they found two angels offering the best news any ears had ever heard.

"He is not here. He is risen."

This gave Mary an amazing opportunity. She became the first person in the world to have the privilege of sharing the news of the resurrection of Christ. This would have never happened for Mary if she hadn't gone. She would have been hiding stuck in the grief. But she went, knowing she still had something she could do. John 20:18 says she ran back to where the disciples were and told them what she had seen and heard.

There is a lesson in here for you and me. Even when all seems lost, it isn't. Even when it seems too late, it's not.

Because that's the power of the resurrection. No matter what life throws your way. You will not be defeated. God can turn your situation around. You can trust Him. He speaks new life into dreams and destinies that seemed lost forever. He takes whatever you have and breathes resurrection life into it, so that it becomes more and does more than you could have ever imagined.

....

Even when all seems lost, it isn't.
Even when it seems too late, it's not.

....

That's the case with all the stories I've shared in this chapter. And when we trust God and move forward, amazing things happen.

Are you looking at what you have lost or trusting God with what you have? God knew everything that would happen to you. He's already written every day of your life in His book. The loss, the disappointment, the bad break is not how your story ends. It may not have been fair, but God knows how to make up for it. He has beauty for ashes, joy for mourning. There are good chapters up ahead but you have to move forward.

Don't get stuck in bitterness, in self-pity and "why me?" Your future is not dependent on what you've lost. The good news is, you are graced to go. God is breathing on your life. Courage is rising up, strength, favor, the right people. He's working all things for your good.

Stay in faith and you'll step into the new things He has in store. This is the encouragement I hope you've taken from every chapter in this book. I hope you now see that "stuck" is not God's destiny for you.

You can be bold and move forward. You are graced to go in the strength you have. Graced to go in whatever position you're in. Graced to go knowing that you matter so very much to your Heavenly Father. Graced to go with eyes to see the good in your life and in others. Graced to go, abundantly releasing your blessing so you can bless others. Graced to go free from the shackles of regret. And as we've seen in this chapter, you are graced to go trusting God.

God is for you. He is with you. And He has provided grace to go! To go into higher. To go into better. To go into a life full of purpose and meaning.

Grace Thoughts

+ When all seems lost, that's the moment I begin to look at what I have, knowing, whatever it is, it's enough.

+ I have a bright future, even when it seems hopeless. I know I have a God with a pen in His hand. I know God isn't finished writing my story.

+ I will not let life steal my hope. I am what God calls me—Blessed, Favored, Victorious, and so much more.

+ When I stay in faith, I will step into the new things God has in store for me.

+ I know when I trust God, He is working in my life. I will come through in victory.

Grace Reflections

1. God asked Craig Johnson, "Do you trust Me?" In my heart of hearts, what is my answer to that same question?

   ....

   ....

2. God is waiting to do something bigger and better in my life. Do I have a sense of what that bigger, better *is*?

   ....

   ....

3. Am I more focused on what I have lost or on what I have?

   ....

   ....

4. God has graced me to go. What is my next step?

   ....

   ....

ACKNOWLEDGMENTS

I have discovered that most accomplishments borne through discipline, patience, and diligent effort are the most satisfying of all. Whether it be a lifetime of faith, the rearing of children, or writing a book, when we put everything we have into something and give it our best effort, we can step back from the finished product and say, "I'm proud of what I've done." The effort we put into everything we do in our life should be as rewarding as the result.

I was blessed to work with so many excellent people; it has been a joyful endeavor and a rewarding one. To all of them I owe my appreciation and gratitude.

First, I want to thank everyone at FaithWords/ Hachette who brought their exceptional talents to this book, especially Daisy Hutton and Beth Adams.

I also want to thank my literary agents Jan Miller and Shannon Marven and the exceptional team at Dupree Miller for their friendship and loyalty and for thinking as big as we do.

When we stay in faith, God always brings the right people across our paths at the appropriate time and season. I would like to thank David Holland for his exceptional insight on this journey.

My warmest gratitude I extend to the Lakewood Church family and our extraordinary staff. Together we are accomplishing the most important mission of all: sharing the love and hope of our Savior with the world.

I am grateful to have grown up in the family God gave to me. My mother, Georgine, and my father, Donald, love me dearly and instilled in me—from the beginning—a sense of purpose and destiny. They took me to church and modeled for me the faith and values that I still possess today. Because of them, I have passed these blessings to my children, as they will do for theirs.

My brother, Donald Jr., is a guiding light in our ministry and in my life. I am grateful for his wisdom, his steadfast support, and his belief in me. I am blessed to have a brother like him.

I cannot sufficiently convey the love and gratitude in my heart for how wonderful and extraordinary my husband and children have made my life. Joel is the love I always hoped for. He is my best friend, and the person who encourages me the most to achieve all that God has planned for me. When God gave to me my children, Jonathan and Alexandra, He placed in my life the very sunshine that rises each day. And as my family grows, I am so grateful for my beautiful daughter-in-law, Sophia. She is kind and loving, and such a wonderful addition to our family. They fill my life with joy, laughter, and love, and they make my life richer.

Finally, and most important, I want to give my eternal gratitude and praise to my Lord and Savior, Jesus Christ. I dedicate this work to Him, because words are only words until He breathes His life into them.

ABOUT THE AUTHOR

Victoria Osteen is the co-pastor of Lakewood Church, the *New York Times* bestselling author of *Love Your Life,* and the host of the national weekly radio program *Victoria Osteen Live* and her weekly podcast *Victoria and Friends* on Joel Osteen Radio, SiriusXM Channel 128. She is an integral part of each service at Lakewood as well as the "Night of Hope" events across the United States and abroad. She lives with her family in Houston, Texas.

SOURCE NOTES

WE WANT TO HEAR FROM YOU!

Each week, Joel closes our international television broadcast by giving the audience an opportunity to make Jesus the Lord of their lives. I'd like to extend that same opportunity to you.

Are you at peace with God? A void exists in every person's heart that only God can fill. I'm not talking about joining a church or finding religion. I'm talking about finding life and peace and happiness. Would you pray with me today? Just say, "Lord Jesus, I repent of my sins. I ask You to come into my heart. I make You my Lord and Savior."

Friend, if you prayed that simple prayer, I believe you have been "born again." I encourage you to attend a good Bible-based church and keep God in first place in your life. For free information on how you can grow stronger in your spiritual life, please feel free to contact us.

Joel and I love you, and we'll be praying for you. We're believing for God's best for you, that you will see your dreams come to pass. We'd love to hear from you!

To contact us, write to:

Joel and Victoria Osteen
PO Box #4271
Houston, TX 77210

Or you can reach us online at joelosteen.com.

Victoria *and* Friends

Featuring intimate and entertaining conversations with well-known guests on topics ranging from maintaining a healthy mind, body & soul, thriving in love and relationships, living with purpose, and more, Victoria & Friends empowers listeners to live every day to its fullest.

Subscribe today to the Victoria Osteen Podcast.

SiriusXM

Stay connected and inspired!

Follow @victoriaosteen on social media.

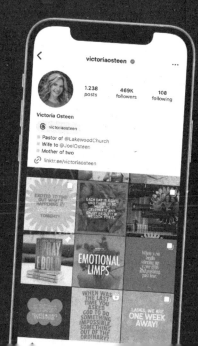

GRACE NOTES